Traefik API Gateway for Microservices

With Java and Python Microservices Deployed in Kubernetes

Rahul Sharma
Akshay Mathur

Apress®

Traefik API Gateway for Microservices

Rahul Sharma
Patpargunj, Delhi, India

Akshay Mathur
Gurgaon, Haryana, India

ISBN-13 (pbk): 978-1-4842-6375-4
https://doi.org/10.1007/978-1-4842-6376-1

ISBN-13 (electronic): 978-1-4842-6376-1

Managing Director, Apress Media LLC: Welmoed Spahr
Acquisitions Editor: Divya Modi
Development Editor: Laura Berendson
Coordinating Editor: Divya Modi

Cover designed by eStudioCalamar

Cover image designed by Freepik (www.freepik.com)

Distributed to the book trade worldwide by Springer Science+Business Media New York, 1 New York Plaza, Suite 4600, New York, NY 10004-1562, USA. Phone 1-800-SPRINGER, fax (201) 348-4505, e-mail orders-ny@springer-sbm.com, or visit www.springeronline.com. Apress Media, LLC is a California LLC and the sole member (owner) is Springer Science + Business Media Finance Inc (SSBM Finance Inc). SSBM Finance Inc is a **Delaware** corporation.

For information on translations, please e-mail booktranslations@springernature.com; for reprint, paperback, or audio rights, please e-mail bookpermissions@springernature.com.

Apress titles may be purchased in bulk for academic, corporate, or promotional use. eBook versions and licenses are also available for most titles. For more information, reference our Print and eBook Bulk Sales web page at http://www.apress.com/bulk-sales.

Any source code or other supplementary material referenced by the author in this book is available to readers on GitHub via the book's product page, located at www.apress.com/978-1-4842-6375-4. For more detailed information, please visit http://www.apress.com/source-code.

Printed on acid-free paper

To our families, for all the personal time spent on this book

Table of Contents

About the Authors

Rahul Sharma is a seasoned Java developer with over 15 years of industry experience. In his career, he has worked with companies of various sizes, from enterprises to start-ups. During this time, he has developed and managed microservices on the cloud (AWS/GCE/DigitalOcean) using open source software. He is an open-source enthusiast and shares his experience at local meetups. He has co-authored *Java Unit Testing with JUnit 5* (Apress, 2017) and *Getting Started with Istio Service Mesh* (Apress, 2019).

Akshay Mathur is a software engineer with 15 years of experience, mostly in Java and web technologies. Most of his career has been spent building B2B platforms for enterprises, dealing with concerns like scalability, configurability, multitenancy, and cloud engineering. He has hands-on experience implementing and operating microservices and Kubernetes in these ecosystems. Currently, he enjoys public speaking and blogging on new cloud-native technologies (especially plain Kubernetes) and effective engineering culture.

About the Technical Reviewer

Brijesh is currently working as a lead consultant. He has more than ten years of experience in software development and providing IT solutions to clients for their on-premise or cloud-based applications, spanning from monoliths to microservice-based architecture.

Acknowledgments

This book would not have been possible without the support of many people. I would like to take this opportunity and express my gratitude to each of them.

I would like to thank Divya Modi for believing in the project and making it work. She has been instrumental in starting the project. Moreover, during the project, her editorial support provided a constant push throughout the process. It would have been difficult to deliver the project without your support.

I would like to thank Celestin Suresh John for providing me this wonderful opportunity. Your guidance made sure that we got the correct path outlined from the start.

I would like to thank Brijesh Pant and Laura C. Berendson for sharing valuable feedback. Your advice has helped to deliver the ideas in a better manner.

I would also like to thank my co-author Akshay Mathur for his knowledge and support. Your experience and willingness have made this a successful project. The brainstorming sessions we had helped to express the ideas.

I wish to thank my parents, my loving and supportive wife, Swati, and my son, Rudra. They are a constant source of encouragement and inspiration. Thanks for providing the time and listening to my gibberish when things were not working according to the plan.

Lastly, I would like to thank my friends, who have been my source of knowledge. The discussion we had often helped me to deliberate on various topics. Often our debates have provided the testbed for evaluations.

—Rahul Sharma

ACKNOWLEDGMENTS

I'd like to express my gratitude to my co-author Rahul Sharma for bringing me on board this project. While we had discussed the possibility, the actual opportunity still came suddenly, and I'd like to thank him for his guidance through the process. It was as fun and nerve-wracking as I'd envisioned, and he had my back the whole way as I channeled my inner Douglas Adams and (to borrow from a great man) enjoyed the sound of deadlines whooshing by.

Divya Modi was a constant source of support and encouragement. She gently helped us stay on track and was a picture of calm and confidence, helping us get to completion. And still entertained multiple last-minute requests as I kept tweaking the title.

To our reviewers, Brijesh Pant and Laura C. Berendson, thank you for all the constructive feedback in making this book better.

I'd also like to thank my ever-patient family, especially my mother, my wife, Neha, and my daughter, Inara, who kept wondering when I would actually be *done* and free to talk to them, as I kept fiddling till the last minute and repeating, "Almost there!".

I'm grateful to the two mentors who pulled me up to the level of authoring a book—Aditya Kalia and Shekhar Gulati.

Finally, our gratitude to the Traefik team for releasing an excellent product to the community. We hope this book helps in any small way to drive further adoption.

—Akshay Mathur

Introduction

Microservice architecture has brought dynamism to the application ecosystem. New services are built and deployed while older ones are deprecated and removed from the enterprise application estate. But front-end load balancers haven't been able to adapt to the components in the enterprise architecture. Most current load balancers have a static configuration. They require configuration updates as the application landscape changes. Thus, there are operational complexities when working with microservices. These are a few of the challenges of getting a microservices-based solution to work. The dynamic nature of the ecosystem requires dynamic tools that can autoconfigure themselves.

Traefik bases its foundations on the dynamic nature of the Microservice architecture. It has built first-class support for service discovery, telemetry, and resiliency. It is a modern HTTP reverse proxy and load balancer that eases microservices deployment. Its integration has been great, with many existing tools.

The book covers Traefik setup, basic workings, and integration with microservices. It is intended for developers, project managers, and DevOps personnel interested in solutions for their operational challenges. The book is not specific to any programming language, even though all the examples use Java or Python.

CHAPTER 1

Introduction to Traefik

Over the last couple of years, microservices have become a mainstream architecture paradigm for enterprise application development. They have replaced the monolithic architecture of application development, which was mainstream for the past couple of decades. Monolithic applications are developed in a modular architecture. This means that discrete logic components, called *modules*, are created to segregate components based on their responsibility. Even though an application consisted of discrete components, they were packaged and deployed as a single executable. Overall, the application has very tight coupling. Changes to each of these modules can't be released independently. You are required to release a complete application each time.

A monolithic architecture is well suited when you are building an application with unknowns. In such cases, you often need quick prototyping for every feature. Monolithic architecture helps in this case, as the application has a unified code base. The architecture offers the following benefits.

- Simple to develop.

- Simple to test. For example, you can implement end-to-end testing by launching the application and testing the UI with Selenium.

- Simple to deploy. You only have to copy the packaged application to a server.

© Rahul Sharma, Akshay Mathur 2021
R. Sharma and A. Mathur, *Traefik API Gateway for Microservices*,
https://doi.org/10.1007/978-1-4842-6376-1_1

- Simple to scale horizontally by running multiple copies behind a load balancer.

In summary, you can deliver the complete application quickly in these early stages. But as the application grows organically, the gains erode. In the later stages, the application becomes harder to maintain and operate. Most of the subcomponents get more responsibility and become large subsystems. Each of these subsystems needs a team of developers for its maintenance. As a result, the complete application is usually maintained by multiple development teams. But the application has high coupling, so development teams are interdependent while making new features available. Due to a single binary, the organization faces the following set of issues.

- **Quarterly releases**: Application features take more time to release. Most of the time, an application feature needs to be handled across various subsystems. Each team can do their development, but deployment requires the entire set of components. Thus, teams can seldom work independently. Releases are often a big coordinated effort across different teams, which can be done only a couple of times per period.

- **Deprecated technology**: Often, when you work with technology, you must upgrade it periodically. The upgrades make sure all vulnerabilities are covered. Application libraries often require frequent upgrades as they add new features as well. But upgrading the libraries in a monolith is difficult. A team can try to use the latest version, but often needs to make sure that the upgrade does not break other subsystems. In certain situations, an upgrade can even lead to a complete rewrite of subsystems, which is a very risky undertaking for the business.

- **Steep learning curve**: Monolithic applications often have a large code base. But the individual developers are often working on a very small subset of the codebase. At first glance, the lines of code create a psychological bottleneck for developers. Moreover, since the application is tightly coupled, developers usually need to know how others invoke the code. Thus, the overall onboarding time for a new developer is large. Even the experienced developers find it hard to make changes to modules that have not been maintained well. This creates a knowledge gap that widens over time.

- **Application scaling**: Typically, a monolithic application can only be scaled vertically. It is possible to scale the application horizontally, but you need to determine how each subsystem maintains its internal state. In any case, the application requires resources for all subsystems. Resources can't be selectively provided to subsystems under load. Thus, it is an all-or-nothing scenario with a monolithic application. This is often a costly affair.

When faced with challenges, organizations look for alternative architectures to address these issues.

Microservice Architecture

Microservice architecture is an alternative to the monolithic architecture (see Figure 1-1). It converts the single application to a distributed system with the following characteristics.

- **Services**: Microservices are developed as services that can work independently and provide a set of business capabilities. A service may depend on other services to perform the required functionality. Independent teams can develop each of these services. The teams are free to select and upgrade the technology they need for their service. An organization often delegates full responsibility for the services to their respective teams. The teams must ensure that their respective service runs as per the agreed availability and meets the agreed quality metrics.

- **Business context**: A service is often created around a business domain. This makes sure that it is not too fine-grained or too big. A service needs to answer first if it is the owner of the said business function or the consumer of the function. A function owner must maintain all the corresponding function data. If it needs some more supporting function, it may consume the same from another service. Thus determining business context boundaries helps keep a check on the service dependencies. Microservices aim to build a system with loose coupling and high cohesion attributes. Aggregating all logically related functionality makes the service an independent product.

- **Application governance**: In enterprise systems, governance plays an important role. You rarely want to make systems that are difficult to run. Due to this, a governance group keeps check on the technologies used by developers so that the operations team can still run the system. But microservice architecture provides the complete ownership to the respective teams. The ownership is not limited to development. It also delegates service operations. Due to this, most organizations must adopt DevOps practices. These practices enable the development teams to operate and govern a service efficiently.

- **Automation**: Automation plays an important role in microservices. It applies to all forms like infrastructure automation, test automation, and release automation. Teams need to operate efficiently. They need to test more often and release quickly. This is only possible if they rely more on machines and less on manual intervention. Post-development manual testing is a major bottleneck. Thus, teams often automate their testing in numerous ways like API testing, smoke testing, nightly tests, and so forth. They often perform exploratory testing manually to validate the build. Release and infrastructure preparation is often automated by using DevOps practices.

 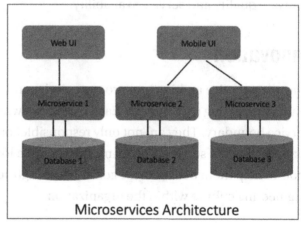

Figure 1-1. *Monolith vs. microservices*

In summary, a monolith has a centralized operating model. This means that all code resides in one place; everyone uses the same library, releases happen simultaneously, and so forth. But on the other end, microservices is a completely decentralized approach. Teams are empowered to make the best decisions with complete ownership. Adopting such an architecture not only asks for a change in software design, but it also asks for a change in organizational interaction. Organizations reap the following benefits of such application design.

Agility

This is one of the biggest driving factors for an organization adopting the microservices architecture. Organizations become more adaptive, and they can respond more quickly to changing business needs. The loose coupling offered by the architecture allows accelerated development. Small, loosely coupled services can be built, modified, and tested individually before deploying them in production. The model dictates small independent development teams working within their defined boundaries. These teams are responsible for maintaining high levels of software quality and service availability.

Innovation

The microservice architecture promotes independent small development teams supporting each service. Each team has ownership within their service boundary. They are not only responsible for development but also for operating the service. The teams thus adopt a lot of automation and tools to help them deliver these goals. These high-level goals drive the engineering culture within the organization.

Moreover, development teams are usually well aware of the shortcomings of their services. Such teams can address these issues using their autonomous decision-making capability. They can fix the issues and improve service quality frequently. Here again, teams are fully empowered to select appropriate tools and frameworks for their purpose. It ultimately leads to the improved technical quality of the overall product.

Resilience

Fault isolation is the act of limiting the impact of a failure to a limited subsystem/component. This principle allows a subsystem to fail as long as it does not impact the complete application. The distributed nature of microservice architecture offers fault isolation, a principal requirement to build resilient systems. Any service which is experiencing failures can be handled independently. Developers can fix issues and deploy new versions while the rest of the application continues to function independently.

Resilience, or *fault tolerance*, is often defined as the application's ability to function properly in the event of a failure of some parts. Distributed systems like microservices are based on various tenets like circuit breaking, throttling to handle fault propagation. This is an important aspect; if done right, it offers the benefits of a resilient system. But if this is left unhandled, it leads to frequent downtime due to failures cascading. Resilience also improves business agility as developers can release new services without worrying about system outages.

Scalability

Scalability is defined as the capability of a system to handle the growth of work. In a monolith, it is easy to quantify the system scalability. In a monolithic system, as the load increases, not all subsystems get proportionally increased traffic. It is often the case that some parts of the system get more traffic than others. Thus, the overall system performance is determined by a subset of the services. It is easier to scale a monolithic system by adding more hardware. But at times, this can also be difficult as different modules may have conflicting resource requirements. Overall an overgrown monolith underutilizes the hardware. It often exhibits degraded system performance.

The decoupling offered by microservices enables the organization to understand the traffic that each microservice is serving. The *divide and conquer* principle helps in improving the overall system performance. Developers can adopt appropriate task parallelization or clustering techniques for each service to improve the system throughput. They can adopt appropriate programming languages and frameworks, fine-tuned with the best possible configuration. Lastly, hardware can be allocated by looking into service demand rather than scaling the entire ecosystem.

Maintainability

Technical debt is a major issue with monolithic systems. Overgrown monoliths often have parts that are not well understood by the complete team. Addressing technical debt in a monolith is difficult as people often fear of breaking any of the working features. There have been cases where unwanted dead code was made alive by addressing technical debt on a particular monolith.

Microservice architecture helps to mitigate the problem by following the principle of divide and conquer. The benefits can be correlated with an object-oriented application design where the system is broken into objects. Each object has a defined contract and thus leads to improved maintenance of the overall system. Developers can unit test each of the objects being refactored to validate the correctness. Similarly, microservices created around a business context have a defined contract. These loosely coupled services can be refactored and tested individually.

Developers can address the technical debt of the service while validating the service contract. Adopting microservices is often referred to as a monolith's *technical debt payment*.

You have looked at the advantages of Microservice architecture. But the architecture also brings a lot of challenges. Some challenges are due to the distributed nature of the systems, while others are caused by diversity in the application landscape. Services can be implemented in different technologies and scaled differently. There can be multiple versions of the same service serving different needs. Teams should strategize to overcome these challenges during application design and not as an afterthought. Application deployment is one such important aspect. Monoliths have been deployed on a three-tier model. But the same model does not work well with microservices. The next section discusses the changes required in the deployment model.

n-Tier Deployment

n-tier deployment is a design implementation where web applications are segregated into application presentation, application processing, and data management functions. These functions are served by independent components known as *tiers*. The application tiers allow segregation of duties. All communication is linear across the tiers. Each tier is managed by its own software subsystem. The *n*-tier deployment offers the benefit of improved scalability of the application. Monolithic applications are usually deployed as three-tiers (see Figure 1-2) applications.

- **Presentation tier**: This tier is responsible for serving all static content of the application. It is usually managed by using web servers like Apache, Nginx, and IIS. These web servers not only serve applications static UI components but also handle dynamic content by routing requests to the application tier. Web servers are optimized to handle many requests for static data. Thus, under load, they perform well. Some of these servers also provide different load balancing mechanisms. These mechanisms can support multiple nodes of the application tier.

- **Application tier**: This tier is responsible for providing all processing functions. It contains the business processing logic to deliver the core capabilities of an application. The development team is responsible for building this in a suitable technology stack like Java, Python, and .NET. This tier is capable of serving a user request and generating an appropriate dynamic response. It receives requests from the presentation tier. To serve the request, the application tier may need additional data to interact with the data tier.

- **Data tier**: This tier provides capabilities of data storage and data retrieval. These data management functions are outside the scope of the application. Thus, an application uses a database to fulfill these needs. The data tier provides data manipulation functions using an API. The application tier invokes this API.

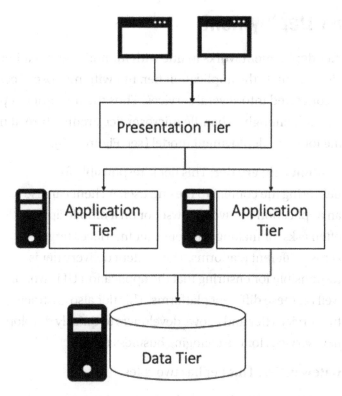

Figure 1-2. *Three-tier*

There are many benefits to using a three-layer architecture, including scalability, performance, and availability. You can deploy the tiers on different machines and can use the available resources in an optimized manner. The application tier delivers most of the processing capability. Thus, it needs more resources. On the other hand, the web servers serve static content and do not need many resources. This deployment model improves application availability by having different replication strategies for each tier.

Four-Tier Deployment

The three-tier deployment works in line with monolith applications. The monolith is usually the application tier. But with microservices, the monolith is converted into several services. Thus the three-tier deployment model is not good enough to handle microservice architecture. It needs the following four-tier deployment model (see Figure 1-3).

- **Content delivery tier**: This tier is responsible for delivering the content to the end user. A client can use an application in a web browser or on a mobile app. It often asks for making different user interfaces targeted across different platforms. The content delivery tier is responsible for ensuring that the application UI is working well on these different platforms. This tier also abstracts the services tier and allows developers to quickly develop new services for the changing business needs.

- **Gateway tier**: This tier has two roles.

  - Dynamically discover the deployed services and correlate them with the user request

  - Route requests to services and send responses

  For each request, the gateway layer receives data from all the underlying services and sends back a single aggregated response. It has to handle different scenarios like role-based access, delayed responses, and error responses. These behaviors make it easier for the service tier. The service tier can focus only on the business requirements.

- **Services tier**: This tier is responsible for providing all business capabilities. The services tier is designed for a microservices approach. This tier provides data to its clients without concern for how it is consumed. The clients can be other services or application UI. Each of the services can be scaled based on their requests load pattern. The clients have the responsibility to determine the new instances. All of this enables a pluggable approach to the application ecosystem. New services can be built by consuming existing services. They can be readily integrated into the enterprise landscape.

- **Data tier**: This tier provides capabilities of data storage and data retrieval. Data management capabilities are still beyond the application scope. But each service has an exclusive data management infrastructure. It can be DBMS like MySQL or a document store like Mongo.

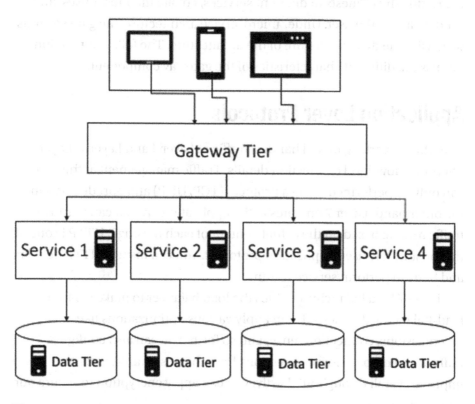

Figure 1-3. *Four-tier*

The four-tier architecture (see Figure 1-3) was pioneered by early microservices adopters like Netflix, Amazon, and Twitter. At the center of the paradigm, the gateway tier is responsible for binding together the complete solution. The gateway needs a solution that can link the remaining tiers together so all of them can communicate, scale, and deliver. In the three-tier architecture, the presentation tier had webservers that can be adopted for the gateway tier. But first, you should determine the characteristics required to be a gateway tier solution.

Gateway Characteristics

A gateway is the point of entry for all user traffic. It is often responsible for delegating the requests to different services, collate their responses, and send it back to the user. Under microservice architecture, the gateway must work with the dynamic nature of the architecture. The following sections discuss the different characteristics of the gateway component.

Application Layer Protocols

The OSI networking model handles traffic at Layer 4 and Layer 7. Layer 4 offers only low-level connection details. Traffic management at this layer can only be performed using a protocol (TCP/UDP) and port details. On the other hand, Layer 7 operates at the application layer. It can perform traffic routing based on the actual content of each message. HTTP is one of the most widely used application protocols. You can inspect HTTP headers and body to perform service routing.

Layer 7 load balancing enables the load balancer to make smarter load-balancing decisions. It can apply various optimizations like compressions, connection reuse, and so forth. You can also configure buffering to offload slow connections from the upstream servers to improve overall throughput. Lastly, you can apply encryption to secure our communication.

In the current ecosystem, there are a wide variety of application protocols to choose from. Each of these protocols serves a set of needs. Teams may adapt a particular application protocol, let's say gRPC because it is better suited for their microservice. This does not require the other teams to adapt to the same application protocol. But in the ecosystem, the gateway needs to delegate traffic to most of these services. Thus, it needs to have support for the required protocol. The list of application protocols is extensive. Consequently, the gateway needs to have a rich set of current protocols. Moreover, it should be easy to extend this list by adding new protocols.

PROTOCOLS

HTTP/2 is the next version of the HTTP/1.1 protocol. It is a binary protocol and does not change any of the existing HTTP semantics. But it offers real-time multiplex communication and improves the application performance by employing better utilization of underlying TCP connections.

gRPC is a binary RPC protocol. It offers various features, such as multiplexing, streaming, health metrics, and connection pooling. It is often used with payload serialization like JSON or protocol buffers.

REST (REpresentational State Transfer) is an application protocol based on HTTP semantics. The protocol represents resources that are accessed using HTTP methods. It is often used with a JSON payload to describe the state.

Another important aspect is the interprocess communication paradigm. Traditionally, we create synchronous applications based on HTTP. But with data-driven microservices, you may want to adopt an asynchronous model, like ReactiveX and Zeromq. A gateway component needs to support both these forms of communication. Developers should be able to pick and choose which model works for their application.

Dynamic Configuration

In a monolith application, you know the location of our backend application. The location does not change often, and more instances of the application are not created at runtime. Since most servers are known, it is easier to provide these details in a static configuration file.

But in a microservices application, that solution does not work. The first challenge arises from the number of microservices. Usually, there are limited services at the start. But as the system grows, people realize there can be multiple fine-grained services for every business function. Often the number can grow to a couple of hundred services. It is a daunting task to allocate a static address to each of these services and maintain the same updates in a static file.

The second challenge arises from scalability offered by microservices. Services can be replicated during load times. These services are removed when the load subsides. This runtime behavior of microservices gets multiplied by the number of services in the ecosystem. It is impossible to keep track of all these changes in a static configuration file.

To solve discovery issues, a microservice architecture advocates a service registry. It is a database containing the network locations of service instances. The service registry needs to be updated in near real time. It needs to reflect the new locations as soon as they are available. A service registry needs to have high availability. Consequently, it consists of a cluster of nodes that replicate data to maintain consistency.

SERVICE REGISTRY PROVIDERS

The following are the most widely used service registry providers.

Eureka is a REST-based solution for registering and querying service instances. Netflix developed the solution as part of its microservices journey. It is often used in the AWS cloud.

etcd is a highly available, distributed, consistent, key-value store. It is used for shared configuration and service discovery. Kubernetes uses etcd for its service discovery and configuration storage.

Consul is a solution for discovering and configuring services created by Hashicorp. Besides the service registry, Consul provides extensive functions like health-checking and locking. Consul provides an API that allows clients to register and discover services.

Apache Zookeeper was created for the Hadoop ecosystem. It is a high-performance coordination service for distributed applications. Curator is a Java library created over Zookeeper to provide service discovery features.

The gateway component needs to interact with the service registry. It can try to poll the service registry, but that is not efficient. Alternatively, the service registry needs to push the changes to the gateway. The gateway needs to pick these changes and reconfigure itself. Thus, in summary, the gateway needs to integrate well with the registry.

Hot Reloads

In a microservice architecture, numerous services are deployed. Each of these existing services may be updated, or new services may be added. All these changes need to be propagated to the gateway tier. Additionally, the gateway component may need some upgrades to address issues. These operations must be performed without making any impact on the end user. A downtime of even a few seconds is detrimental. If the gateway requires downtime for service updates, then the downtime gets multiplied by the frequency of service updates. In summary, this can lead to frequent service outages.

The gateway component should handle all updates without requiring any restart. It must not make any kind of distinction between configuration update or upgrade.

17

Observability

Observability is a concept borrowed from control theory. It is the process of knowing the state of the system while being outside the system. It is about all information you need to diagnose failures. Observability in microservices is completely different from the one in monolith systems. In monolith applications, there is a three-tier deployment with the following logs.

- Request log

- Application log

- Error log

You can connect back the logs to determine (with fair accuracy) what the system had been performing. But in a microservice architecture, there are tens or hundreds of different services you need to keep track of. Using only logs to predict the application state is no longer possible. We need new mechanisms for this purpose. The microservice architecture recommends the following methods.

Tracing

Request tracing is a method to profile and monitor distributed architectures such as microservices. In microservices, a user request is typically handled by multiple services. Each of these services performs its respective processing. All of this is recorded in the form of request-spans. All these spans of a request are combined into a single trace for the entire request. Thus, request tracing shows the time spent by each service for a particular request.

Any service failure can easily be seen in a request trace. The trace also helps in determining performance bottlenecks. Tracing is a great solution for debugging application behavior, but it comes at the cost of consistency. All services must propagate proper request spams. If a service does not provide a span or regenerates the span by neglecting the existing headers, then the resultant request trace is not able to capture the said service.

18

The gateway component receives all traffic from outside the microservices ecosystem. It may distribute the request across different services. Thus, the gateway component needs to generate request spans for tracing.

Metrics

Microservice best practices recommend generating application metrics that can be analyzed. These metrics project the state of our services. Over time, collecting metrics helps with analyzing and improving service performance. In failure scenarios, metrics help determine the root cause. Application-level metrics can include the number of queued inbound HTTP requests, request latency, database connections, and the cache hit ratio. Applications must also create custom metrics that are specific to their context. The gateway component must also export relevant metrics that can be captured. The metrics can be around Status code across different application protocols like HTTP(2XX,4XX,3XX,5XX), service error rates, request queue, and so forth.

In summary, the gateway component needs to offer a wide variety of observability output. It must export stats, metrics, and logs to integrate with monitoring solutions in the microservice architecture.

TLS termination

Data security is often a non-functional requirement of a system. Applications have been achieving data security using TLS communication. TLS communication allows data to be encrypted/decrypted using private-public key pairs. The process of TLS termination at the gateway or presentation tier enables applications to perform better as applications do not have to handle the encryption and decryption themselves. This worked well in traditional architectures as the interprocess network calls were minimal. But in a microservice architecture, many services are running in the ecosystem. As per security standards, unencrypted communication between services presents a grave risk. Thus, as a best practice, you are required to encrypt all network communication throughout the cluster.

Service authorization is another challenge in a microservice architecture. In microservices, many more requests are made over the network. A service needs to make sure which client is making invocations. This helps place limits if the client service is malfunctioning. Putting these controls is necessary as a rouge service and wreak havoc in the system. Identity can be established in many ways. Clients can pass bearer tokens, but this process is outdated. Bearer tokens can be captured and passed by a potential attacker. As a best practice, you want to ensure that clients are only authenticated using non-portable identities. Mutual TLS (mTLS) authentication is thus a recommended practice. For services to authenticate with each other, they each need to provide a certificate and key that the other trusts before establishing a connection. This action of both the client and server providing and validating certificates is referred to as mutual TLS. It ensures that strong service identities are enforced and exchanged as part of interprocess communication. Thus, the gateway component needs to have dual behaviors.

- TLS termination for traffic from the outside world

- TLS identity for invoking different services using mutual TLS

Other Features

The gateway component performs the dual responsibilities of a reverse proxy and a load balancer. It must provide support for advanced load balancing techniques. Moreover, the component needs to support the following features.

- Timeouts and retries

- Rate limiting

- Circuit breaking

- Shadowing and buffering

- Content-based routing

The list of features is not limited. Load balancers often implement various security features like authentication and DoS mitigation using IP address tagging and identification and tarpitting. The gateway components must address all these needs as well.

We have discussed the high-level behaviors expected from a gateway solution. These needs were a wish list from established market products like Apache, Nginx, and HAProxy. These servers provide support for a few features, but some of the features have to be handled using workarounds. In summary, these battle-tested solutions do not have first-class support for microservice architecture. These products had developed their architectures a decade back when the list of requirements was different. The next section discusses Traefik, an open source product created to handle microservices deployment needs.

Traefik

Traefik is an open source API gateway. It was designed to simplify complexity regarding microservices operations. Traefik achieves the same by performing autoconfiguration of services. As per the product documentation, developers should be responsible for developing services and deploying them. Traefik can autoconfigure itself with sensible defaults and send a request to the said service.

Today's microservices have changing needs. Traefik supports all these needs by following a pluggable architecture. It supports every major cluster technology such as Kubernetes, Docker, Docker Swarm, AWS, Mesos, and Marathon (see Figure 1-4). All these engines have their own integration points, also known as *providers*. There is no need to maintain a static configuration file. The provider is responsible for connecting to the orchestration engine and determining the services running on it. It then passes this information back to the Traefik server, which can apply this to its routing. Traefik is capable of integrating with multiple providers at the same time.

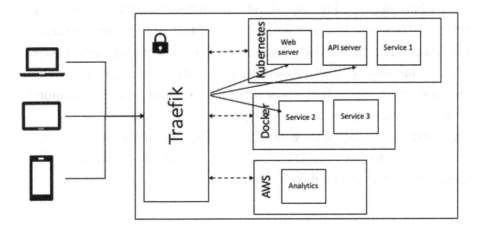

Figure 1-4. *Traefik*

Traefik was developed in a Unix-centric way. It was built in Golang. It delivers a fair performance. It has seen some memory issues. But there is a large community of active developers working on Traefik. The overall performance offered by Traefik is a little less than the established market leaders like Nginx, but it makes up for it by providing first-class support for all microservices features.

Note   Traefik has more than 25K GitHub stars (at the time of writing), making it one of the most actively viewed projects.

Installation

Traefik is released often. Binary artifacts for these releases are available on the project release page (`https://github.com/containous/traefik/releases`). The product is released for every supported OS and architecture. At the time of writing, the book Traefik 2.2.0 was the latest release (see Figure 1-5).

Figure 1-5. *Traefik release page*

For the remainder of the chapter, we work with a macOS version, but you can download a suitable release using any of the following methods.

- Open `https://github.com/containous/traefik/releases` and click the release. `traefik_v2.2.0_darwin_amd64.tar.gz`

- Execute the `curl` command for the terminal: `curl -o https://github.com/containous/traefik/releases/download/v2.2.0/traefik_v2.2.0_darwin_amd64.tar.gz`

- Unpack the archive: `tar -zxvf traefik_v2.2.0_darwin_amd64.tar.gz`

- The folder should contain the `traefik` executable, along with two more files.

```
$ ls -al
total 150912
-rw-rw-r--@  1 rahulsharma  staff  551002    Mar 25 22:38 CHANGELOG.md
-rw-rw-r--@  1 rahulsharma  staff  1086      Mar 25 22:38 LICENSE.md
-rwxr-xr-x@  1 rahulsharma  staff  76706392 Mar 25 22:55 traefik
```

The single binary provides a simplified and streamlined experience while working across different platforms. Let's now learn how to work with Traefik.

Traefik Command Line

Traefik can be started by invoking the `traefik` command. The single command can do any of the following.

- Configure Traefik based on the provided configuration

- Determine the Traefik version

- Perform health-checks on Traefik

It is important to understand how the traefik command supports each of these behaviors. There are several parameters offered in the traefik command. You will work with them once we reach the relevant topics. As a first step, let's validate the version of Traefik by executing the following command.

```
$ ./traefik version
Version:      2.2.0
Codename:     chevrotin
Go version:   go1.14.1
Built:        2020-03-25T17:17:27Z
OS/Arch:      darwin/amd64
```

This output not only shows the Traefik version, but it also shows information related to the platform and the date on which the Traefik binary was created. In general, the traefik command has the following syntax.

```
traefik [sub-command] [flags] [arguments]
```

In this command, all arguments are optional. Now you configure Traefik by invoking the command. It is important to note that Traefik configuration can be provided in the following ways.

- A configuration file

- User-specified command-line flags

- System environment variables

They are evaluated in the order listed. Traefik applies a default value if no value is specified. You can execute the command without passing any of these values.

```
$ ./traefik
INFO[0000] Configuration loaded from flags.
```

This output tells you that Traefik has started. It is configured with flag-based configuration. The command starts listening on port 80. Let's now validate this by doing a cURL for http://localhost/.

```
$ curl -i http://localhost/
HTTP/1.1 404 Not Found
Content-Type: text/plain; charset=utf-8
X-Content-Type-Options: nosniff
Date: Fri, 01 May 2020 16:16:32 GMT
Content-Length: 19

404 page not found
```

The cURL request gets a 404 response from the server. We revisit the configuration details in the next chapters when we discuss entry-points, routers, and services.

Traefik API

Traefik also provides the REST API, which accesses all the information available in Traefik. Table 1-1 describes a few major endpoints.

Table 1-1. *API Endpoints in Traefik*

Endpoint	Description
/api/version	Provides information about the Traefik version
/api/overview	Provides statistics about HTTP and TCP along with the enabled features and providers
/api/entrypoints	Lists all the entry points information.
/api/http/services	Lists all the HTTP services information
/api/http/routers	Lists all the HTTP router information
/api/http/middlewares	Lists all the HTTP middlewares information

The full list of APIs is available at traefik.io/v2.2/ operations/ api/#endpoints. The API is disabled by default. It needs to be enabled by passing appropriate flags. You can activate the API by starting Traefik with api.insecure flag, which deploys the REST API as a Traefik endpoint.

```
rahulsharma$ ./traefik -api.insecure true
INFO[0000] Configuration loaded from flags.
```

Now let's do a lookup for http://localhost:8080/api/overview in the browser. The output shows statistics returned from the API (see Figure 1-6).

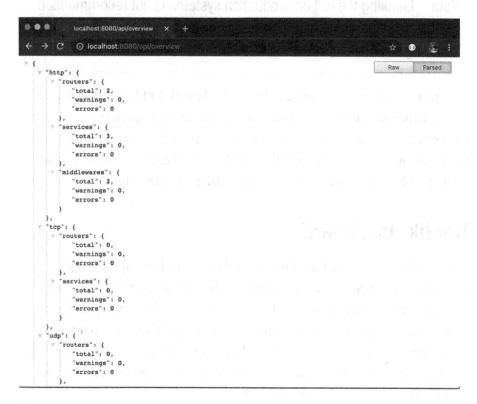

Figure 1-6. *API overview output*

The behavior can also be achieved by using TRAEFIK_API_INSECURE environment variable. The environment variable is equivalent to api. insecure flag. Let's run the command again by setting the environment variable.

```
rahulsharma$ export TRAEFIK_API_INSECURE=True
rahulsharma$ ./traefik
INFO[0000] Configuration loaded from environment variables.
```

Note   Enabling the API on production systems is not recommended. The API can expose complete infrastructure and service details, including sensitive information.

The preceding command deployed the Traefik API in an insecure mode. This is not recommended. Traefik should be secured by authentication and authorization. Moreover, the API endpoint should only be accessible within the internal network and not exposed to the public network. The book covers these practices in further chapters.

Traefik Dashboard

Traefik API comes out of the box with a dashboard (see Figure 1-7). The dashboard is for viewing purposes only. It displays the status of all components configured in Traefik. The dashboard also displays how each of these deployed components is performing. The dashboard is a visual representation that can be used by operation teams for monitoring purposes. Once you have started Traefik in an insecure manner, look up http://localhost:8080/dashboard#/.

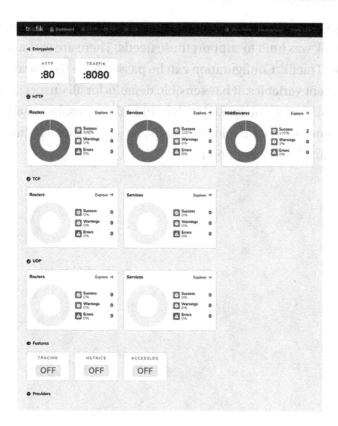

Figure 1-7. *Traefik dashboard*

The dashboard shows TCP and UDP services. There are two listening ports with HTTP-based applications. The dashboard also captures the error rate from each service.

Summary

In this chapter, you looked at how the adoption of microservices has changed the requirements from a gateway. We discussed the various behaviors expected from a gateway component. Established market products like Nginx and HAProxy have tried to adapt these features.

But these products have been unable to provide first-class support of all needs. Traefik was built to support these needs. There are various ways to configure Traefik. Configuration can be passed from file, parameters, or environment variables. It has sensible defaults for all unspecified configuration. Lastly, you looked at the API and the dashboard available in Traefik. Since we have deployed Traefik, let's configure it in the next chapter to handle a few endpoints.

CHAPTER 2

Configure Traefik

In the last chapter, you looked at how the adoption of microservices has changed the requirements of behaviors expected from a gateway component. Traefik was built to support all these needs. There are various ways to configure Traefik; configuration can be passed from a file, parameters, or environment variables. It has sensible defaults for all unspecified configuration. You also looked at the API and the dashboard available in Traefik. In this chapter, let's build upon where you left off by taking a deep dive into various ways to configure Traefik to expose a few endpoints.

This chapter covers the basics of routing. It discusses the various components used in routing. We introduce a small sample application that you use throughout this chapter. The Traefik routing configuration is applied to expose this application to the external world. In this chapter, you try to manually configure Traefik to expose a simple service. In later chapters, you can build upon this to leverage Traefik's autoconfiguration capabilities.

Configuration Topics

Let's cover the following Traefik configuration to expose a sample application on the Traefik gateway.

- Entrypoints

- Providers

© Rahul Sharma, Akshay Mathur 2021
R. Sharma and A. Mathur, *Traefik API Gateway for Microservices*,
https://doi.org/10.1007/978-1-4842-6376-1_2

- Routers

  - Rules

  - Middleware

- Services

The interaction between these configuration pieces is shown in Figure 2-1. We describe each in detail as you move forward.

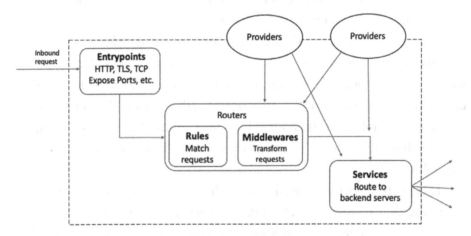

Figure 2-1. *Traefik configuration architecture*

Introduction to Sample Web Service

Before proceeding to the Traefik configuration, let's look at the sample application to expose in Traefik. We use this simple web API throughout this chapter to serve traffic through Traefik.

This simple service is written in Go (as shown in Listing 2-1) and listens on HTTP port 9080. It returns a "Hello World" string on the default path "/".

Listing 2-1. Simple Web API Written in Go

main.go

```go
package main

import (
"fmt"
"log"
"net/http"
)

func main() {
http.HandleFunc("/", handler)
log.Println("Server listening on port 9080...")
log.Fatal(http.ListenAndServe(":9080", nil))
}

func handler(w http.ResponseWriter, r *http.Request) {
fmt.Fprintf(w, "Hello, World")
}
```

Note   You need to have Go 1.1.3 installed on your system to run this example. However, it does not need any other special requirements apart from that. A discussion of Go installation and execution is beyond the scope of this book; however, the official Go documentation is very comprehensive.

In the last chapter, you saw how to install and set up Traefik in stand-alone mode on the machine. Here, you use Traefik CLI. All the examples in this chapter are run on macOS. However, you should be able to easily follow along if you have Go and Traefik CLI installed.

When you run the Go service, you see the console message in Listing 2-2.

Listing 2-2. Running the Go web API

→ **hello-world-service›** `go run main.go`
`2020/05/02 20:34:26 Server listening on port 9080...`

When you open this URL in the browser, you see the following (see Figure 2-2).

Figure 2-2. *Screenshot of browser open to URL http://localhost:9080/*

And you see the following with `curl` on the command line (see Listing 2-3).

Listing 2-3. Testing the API endpoint with curl

→ **hello-world-service›** `curl localhost:9080`
`Hello, World`

For the rest of this chapter, we run this sample application and configure Traefik to expose this application's endpoint. In the course of this, we explore the various Traefik configuration pieces.

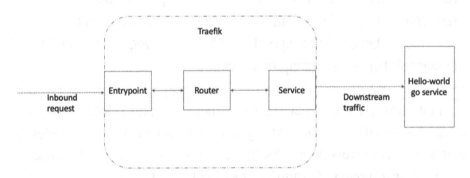

Figure 2-3. *Exposing "Hello World" Go service on Traefik*

Note   For the rest of this chapter, the terms *upstream* and *downstream* describe directional requirements in relation to the message flow: all messages flow from upstream to downstream. The terms *inbound* and *outbound* describe directional requirements in relation to the request route: *inbound* means toward the origin server and *outbound* means toward the user agent. This is per the HTTP specification RFC 7230 Section 2.3 (`https://tools.ietf.org/html/rfc7230#section-2.3`).

Traefik Configuration

Traefik has two ways of providing configuration: static and dynamic (see Figure 2-4).

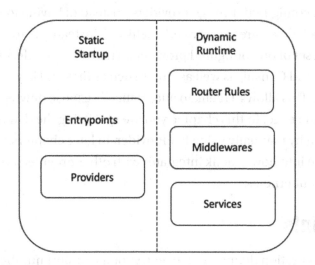

Figure 2-4. Different configuration types in Traefik

Static configuration is provided at startup time through the following mechanisms. It does not change once Traefik starts up.

- File
- CLI
- Environment variables

For static configuration, you configure Traefik first through CLI, then environment variables, and finally, static file configuration.

You define entrypoints in a static configuration—a file or CLI. Entrypoints are the port definition for the ports on which Traefik listens for incoming TCP/UDP traffic.

Providers are the other part of the puzzle which must be specified in a static startup configuration. Providers give Traefik its power. Dynamic configuration, such as routers and services, is changed and refreshed at runtime and configured through providers. Instead of having to manually configure each downstream service, Traefik can instead talk to your service catalog via a set of preconfigured providers. There are providers for Docker, Kubernetes, and Consul, as well as stores such as files and key-value stores such as etcd. This allows Traefik to automatically expose downstream services on the edge. In this chapter, you are specifying the dynamic configuration by manually using FileProvider. In later chapters, you take a deeper dive into how Traefik integrates with other providers, such as Consul and Kubernetes.

Entrypoints

Traefik configuration defines a set of entrypoints (or port numbers) where incoming requests are listened for. These entrypoints can serve HTTP, TLS, gRPC, or TCP traffic. You can define an entrypoint for each backend service you want to expose through the Traefik edge gateway. Entrypoints define the low-level details of addresses, protocols, headers, transport details such as timeouts, and TLS details.

Before you get started defining the entrypoints, let's first revisit how you want to run Traefik and establish how you are observing the defined configuration at runtime. You start Traefik from the command line without any other configuration. To observe the results of the configuration in further steps, you also enable the Traefik web dashboard by passing the '--api.dashboard=true' flag.

Starting Traefik with CLI Arguments

Listing 2-4. Start Traefik with command line arguments

```
→ ~ ./traefik --api.dashboard=true --api.insecure=true
INFO[0000] Configuration loaded from flags.
```

Listing 2-4 starts up Traefik on localhost on port 8080 with the Traefik dashboard exposed with the default configuration. The dashboard is served up under the /api/dashboard/ route.

By default, Traefik recommends exposing the dashboard in secure mode; since you just want to see the dashboard right now without much configuration, you start it in insecure mode with the '--api. insecure=true' flag. Note that this is not recommended for a production use case.

As you can see in Figure 2-5, the Traefik dashboard has a set of sections that allow you to observe all the capabilities configured and enabled in Traefik. Currently, only the default configuration is exposed yet in the Traefik instance.

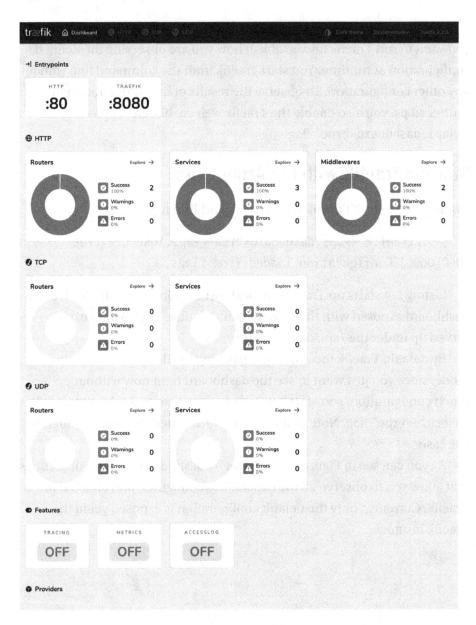

Figure 2-5. *Screenshot of Traefik dashboard open on* `http://` `localhost:8080/`

There are two entrypoints defined by default.

- A default HTTP entrypoint listening on port 80

- An entrypoint named Traefik listening on port 8080 which provides access to the dashboard

The dashboard is not exposed via any special mechanism. Traefik exposes it using a standard entrypoint configuration. Below the entrypoints, you see the routers, middleware, and services categorized by protocol—HTTP, TCP, and UDP. As you move forward, you drill down into these further sections you see on the dashboard.

As you can see, there a bunch of entrypoints, routers, middleware, and services defined by Traefik. The next step is to expose a downstream service using these same mechanisms.

As you have seen, by default Traefik already listens on port 80 (default HTTP) and 8080 (dashboard HTTP) when you enable the web dashboard.

Let's define the own entrypoint to expose the "Hello World" Go service already discussed through Traefik.

First, you need to define an entrypoint. This is done at startup time in a static configuration using one of the following approaches.

- CLI arguments

- Environment variables

- Configuration file traefik.yml in the current directory

Starting Traefik with Entrypoint Defined with CLI

Listing 2-5. Traefik entrypoint defined through command line argument

```
➜  ~ ./traefik --api.dashboard=true --api.insecure=true
--entryPoints.web.address=:80
INFO[0000] Configuration loaded from flags.
```

Listing 2-5 defines an entrypoint called the web that listens on port 80. This overrides the default HTTP entrypoint that you saw earlier on port 80 (see Figure 2-6).

Figure 2-6. *Entrypoints in Traefik dashboard open on* `http://localhost:8080/`

When you try accessing this port on the localhost from cURL, you see the output in Listing 2-6. Traefik is listening to this port, but there is no service at the backend connected to this port yet.

Listing 2-6. Testing the localhost 80 port with curl

```
→ hello-world-service> curl localhost
404 page not found
```

We successfully exposed the entrypoint using command-line parameters to define the static configuration. Next, let's try doing the same using environment variables.

Starting Traefik with Entrypoint Defined in Environment Variables

You execute the following commands in the terminal to start up Traefik with an entrypoint named web exposed on port 80 (see Listing 2-7).

Listing 2-7. Starting Traefik with entrypoint configuration in environment variables

```
→ traefik-config> export TRAEFIK_API_DASHBOARD=true
→ traefik-config> export TRAEFIK_API_INSECURE=true
→ traefik-config> export TRAEFIK_ENTRYPOINTS_WEB_ADDRESS=":80"
→ traefik-config> traefik
INFO[0000] Configuration loaded from environment variables.
```

When you access this endpoint in the browser, you see the same results as before (see Figure 2-7).

Figure 2-7. *No backend service connected to port 80 yet*

Command-line arguments and environment variables are fine to play around with; however, for the rest of this chapter, you are providing all configuration via files. This is the recommended way to configure Traefik as file configuration is simple and less prone to typos and errors. It can also be tracked easily in source control, enabling more of a GitOps model. Next, let's see how to achieve that.

Entrypoint Defined with Config File Traefik.yml in the Current Directory

The Traefik static configuration file can be supplied in multiple ways.

- Traefik.yml file in the current directory
- Traefik.yml file in $HOME/.config

- Location of the file passed in as a command-line argument to the CLI

  ```
  --configFile=path/to/traefik-static-config.yml
  ```

For simplicity, we restrict the Traefik configuration file to the current directory for the rest of this chapter.

TOML vs. YAML

There are two competing formats to define file configuration in Traefik: TOML and YAML.

While the Traefik team prefers TOML, all the configuration examples in this chapter are in YAML. TOML is a lesser-known and obscure format, while YAML is widely supported in various platforms and is the default declarative state configuration format for both the Docker and Kubernetes ecosystems. Instead of learning a new format for defining simple configuration, let's stick to YAML for all needs. YAML has full-feature parity with TOML in all matters of Traefik configuration.

The traefik.yml file in the current directory specifies the entrypoint, as shown in Listing 2-8. You also add the configuration to enable the dashboard here in this file instead of enabling it in the command line.

Listing 2-8. Traefik Static YAML Configuration

```
# Entrypoints have to be defined as static configuration in
traefik.yml
entryPoints:
  web:
    address: ":80"

api:
  insecure: true
  dashboard: true
```

For comparison, the same configuration in TOML format is defined in Listing 2-9. You do not use this; it is just included for reference.

Listing 2-9. Traefik Static TOML Configuration

```
# Entrypoints have to be defined as static configuration in
traefik.yml
[entryPoints]
  [entryPoints.web]
  address = ":80"

[api]
insecure = true
dashboard = true
```

Let's now start up Traefik with the static YAML configuration.

Listing 2-10. Startup Traefik with static file configuration

```
→ traefik-config> ./traefik
INFO[0000] Configuration loaded from file: /Users/akshay/
traefik-book/traefik-config/traefik.yml
```

When you start up Traefik (see Listing 2-10), it automatically picks up the traefik.yml file in the current directory. The result of this is the same as seen in the previous two subsections.

Routers

For each entrypoint exposed by Traefik, corresponding routers must be attached to route traffic flow further. Routers consist of two components.

- A set of rules. Each incoming request on an entrypoint is matched against this set of rules.

- A set of middleware. Each request matched by a rule
  can be transformed using a corresponding middleware.
  Middleware is where all the specialized gateway
  capabilities of authentication and rate limiting are
  carried out.

Now that the entrypoint is exposed, connect the backend Go API to the entrypoint using router configuration. Let's first look at the default routers defined in the Traefik dashboard.

There are two HTTP routers defined by default. When you click 'Explore ->' in the Routers section on the main page, you see the what's shown in Figure 2-8.

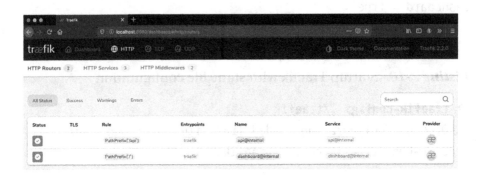

Figure 2-8. *Drill down to default HTTP routers.*

- The first route defined under '/api' is the default parent
  route named api@internal.

- The second route under '/' is the dashboard route
  named 'dashboard@internal.'

You can drill down further into these routers and check their details (see Figures 2-9 and 2-10). These routes serve the traffic for the API and dashboard, respectively.

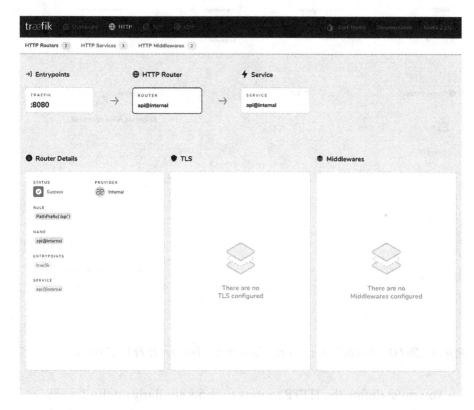

Figure 2-9. *Detail view of api@internal HTTP router*

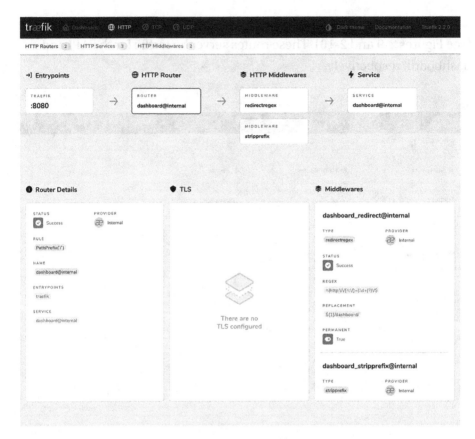

Figure 2-10. *Detail view of dashboard@internal HTTP router*

You must define the HTTP routers to show similarly on the Traefik dashboard. From this point onward, you are leveraging the FileProvider to specify the dynamic configuration. Traefik can talk to the service discovery mechanism of your platform through supported providers. For the simple use case, you are specifying all the configuration in a file, which is easily supported by Traefik. All configuration for routers, middleware, and services is specified through dynamic configuration. There are two ways to specify the FileProvider configuration.

- The individual file specified through the filename

- The entire directory of configuration files, which is the
  recommended method in production because you can
  divide up the various configurations into multiple files

In Listing 2-11, you specify a single filename in the current directory
where you put all the dynamic configurations. Traefik then watches this
file for any changes, and configuration is refreshed automatically within
Traefik.

Listing 2-11. Dynamic configuration file name defined in static
cofiguration

```
# Entrypoints have to be defined as static configuration in
traefik.yml
entryPoints:
  web:
    address: ":80"

providers:
  file:
    filename: "traefik-dynamic-conf.yml"
    watch: true

api:
  insecure: true
  dashboard: true
```

Router Rules

In the traefik-dynamic-conf.yml dynamic configuration file, you first define
the HTTP router and its routing rule (see Listing 2-12).

Listing 2-12. traefik-dynamic-conf.yml dynamic configuration file

```
http:
  routers:
    router0:
      entryPoints:
      - web
      service: hello-world
      rule: Path(`/hello-world`)
```

Once all the configuration is set up, you run Traefik CLI in the same directory (see Listing 2-13).

Listing 2-13. Running Traefik with router rule in dynamic configuration file

```
→ traefik-config› ./traefik
INFO[0000] Configuration loaded from file: /Users/akshay/code/
k8s/traefik-book/traefik-config/traefik.yml
ERRO[2020-05-13T09:22:17+05:30] the service "hello-world@file"
does not exist entryPointName=web routerName=router0@file
ERRO[2020-05-13T09:22:18+05:30] the service "hello-world@file"
does not exist entryPointName=web routerName=router0@file
```

You defined a rule to match a request path (/hello-world) to a backend service that is not yet configured, so Traefik throws up a console error on startup. You see a similar error in the dashboard (see Figure 2-11). The HTTP router section shows an error. Also of interest is the Providers section at the bottom of the page, which now has an entry for FileProvider.

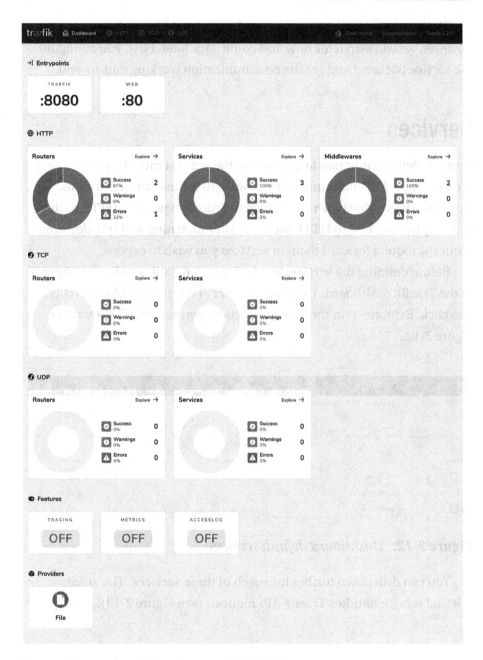

Figure 2-11. Dashboard view with HTTP router

The next piece of the router to configure should be middleware; however, we will skip it for now and come back later. First, you configure the service backend and get the communication working end-to-end.

Services

Services define the actual targets where the request must be routed. They are the actual API endpoints that you want to expose through Traefik. Note that the service type must match the router type (e.g., HTTP router can only be attached to HTTP service). After matching and transforming requests, routers forward them to services you wish to expose.

Before defining the service, let's look at the default services configured in the Traefik dashboard. There are three HTTP services defined. When you click 'Explore ->' in the Services section, you see what's shown in Figure 2-12.

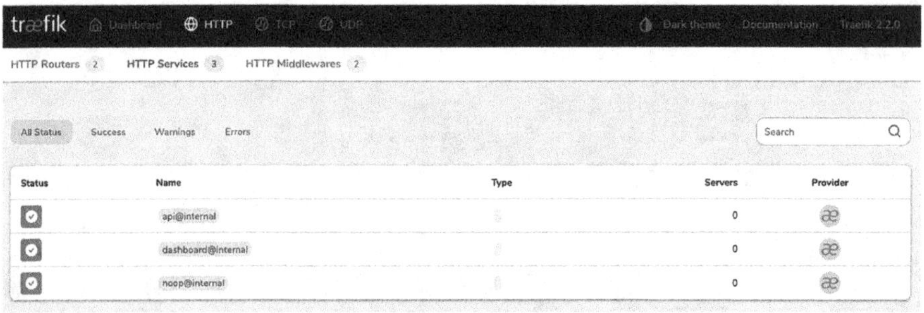

Figure 2-12. *Dashboard default services*

You can drill down further into each of these services. The api@ internal service handles Traefik API requests (see Figure 2-13).

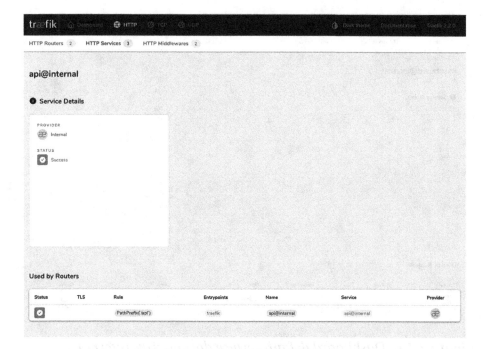

Figure 2-13. *Dashboard default service api@internal*

The dashboard@internal service (see Figure 2-14) handles dashboard requests. Both services are implicitly registered by Traefik when the API and dashboard are enabled.

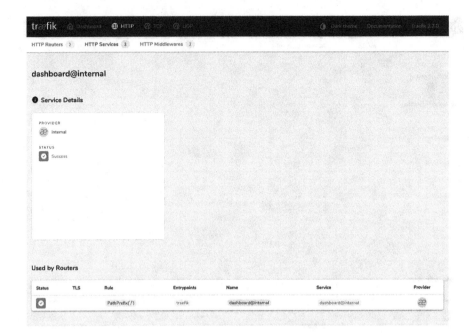

Figure 2-14. *Dashboard default service dashboard@internal*

There is also a noop@internal (as seen in Figure 2-15) which is used in redirection.

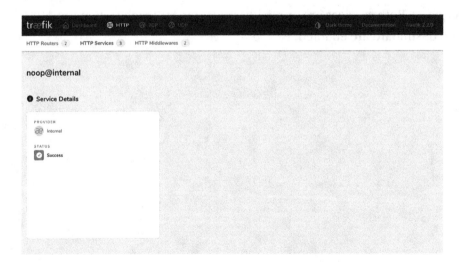

Figure 2-15. *Dashboard default service noop@internal*

Listing 2-14 defines a backend service in traefik-dynamic-conf.yml to fulfill the rule set up in the previous section to route traffic to the Go "Hello World" service. Please recall that the service runs on localhost port 9080.

Listing 2-14. Service configuration in dynamic configuration file

```
# Dynamic configuration
http:
  routers:
    router0:
      entryPoints:
      - web
      service: hello-world
      rule: Path(`/hello-world`)

  services:
    hello-world:
      loadBalancer:
        servers:
        - url: http://localhost:9080/
```

You now start up Traefik and try to access the Go service on the Traefik port 80 on the subpath '/hello-world'. When you use a curl, you see the output in Listing 2-15.

Listing 2-15. Access service endpoint on localhost with curl

➜ **traefik-config›** curl localhost/hello-world
Hello, World

You have now successfully exposed the backend service on port 80 in Traefik. Let's look at what shows up in the Traefik dashboard. You see the HTTP routers, services, and middleware on the main dashboard page (see Figure 2-16).

Figure 2-16. *Router and service configured*

You can drill down to the HTTP services page where you see a new entry for the hello-world service (see Figure 2-17).

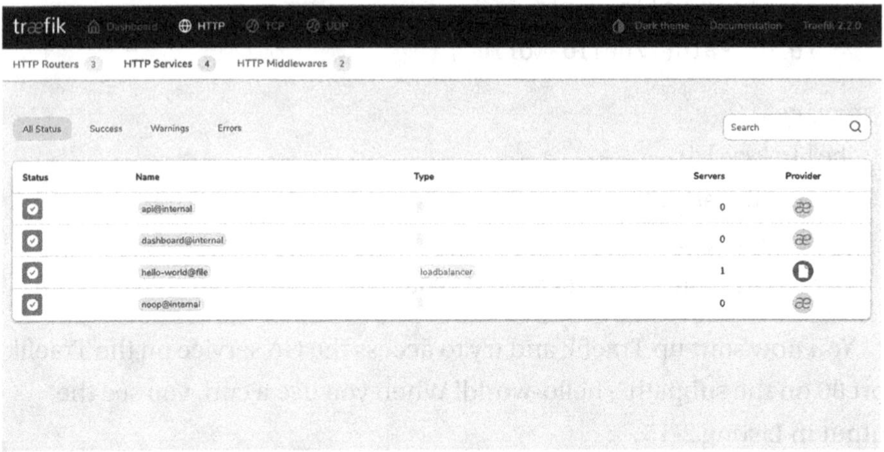

Status	Name	Type	Servers	Provider
✓	api@internal		0	æ
✓	dashboard@internal		0	æ
✓	hello-world@file	loadbalancer	1	O
✓	noop@internal		0	æ

Figure 2-17. *Drill down to configured HTTP services.*

You can then drill down to the hello-world service to view its details (see Figure 2-18). This also shows the backend service URL in the Servers section.

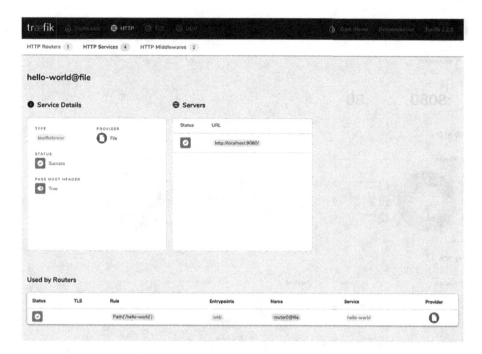

Figure 2-18. *Drill down to configured Hello World file HTTP service*

You then navigate back to the main Dashboard page (see Figure 2-19).

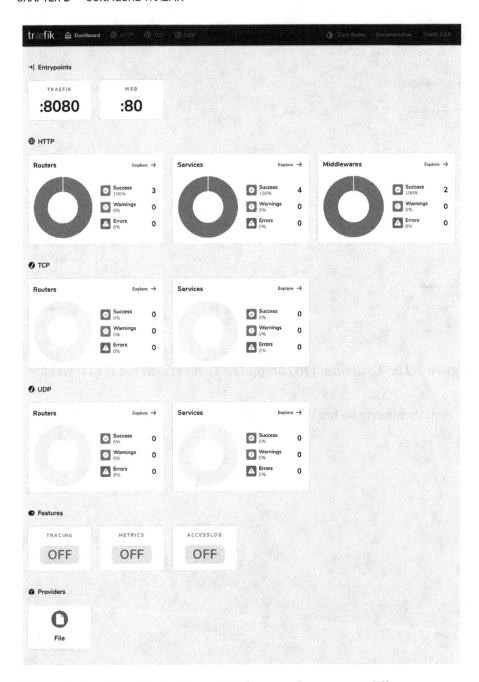

Figure 2-19. *Traefik dashboard before configuring middleware*

From here, you can drill down to the HTTP routers (see Figure 2-20).

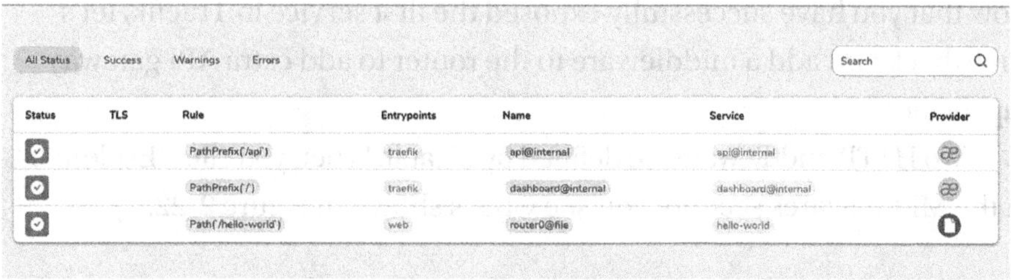

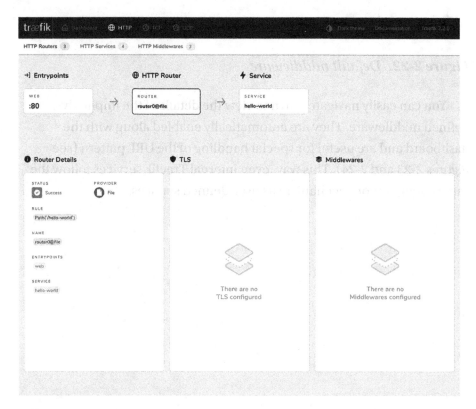

Figure 2-20. *Drill down to configured HTTP routers*

You can then drill down to the HTTP router, which attaches the hello-world service to the web entrypoint (see Figure 2-21).

Figure 2-21. *HTTP router connected to hello-world service*

Middleware

Now that you have successfully exposed the first service in Traefik, let's circle back and add a middleware to the router to add extra API gateway capabilities.

Two HTTP middleware are defined by default. When you click 'Explore ->' in the Middlewares section, you see what's shown in Figure 2-22.

Figure 2-22. *Default middleware*

You can easily navigate down to view the details of the implicitly defined middleware. They are automatically enabled along with the dashboard and are useful for special handling of the URL pattern (see Figures 2-23 and 2-24). This way, even internal Traefik services follow the same configuration mechanism as user-defined services.

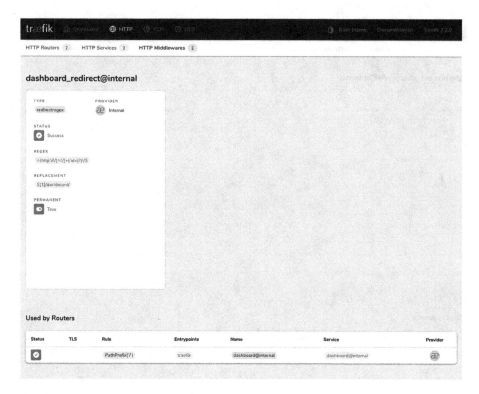

Figure 2-23. *Default dashboard redirect middleware*

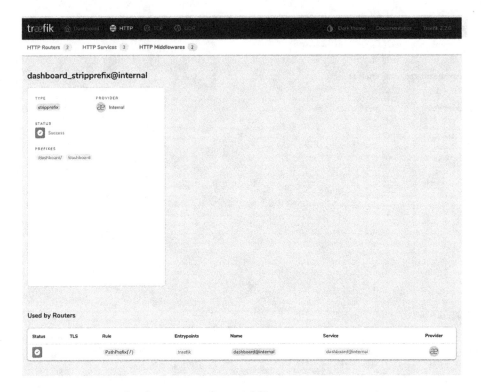

Figure 2-24. *Default stripprefix middleware*

For the use case, you define the built-in basic auth middleware to protect the Hello World API.

Let's start by generating a username-password pair using the htpasswd command-line tool. This is the recommended method on the basic auth page in the Traefik documentation. If you do not have this tool on your system, you can use any other compliant password hashing utility. You use *admin* as username and *admin@123* as the password. The username can be specified as plain-text, but the password must be supplied hashed in MD5, SH1, or BCrypt format (see Listing 2-16).

Listing 2-16. Generate username password pair for authentication

→ **traefik-config›** htpasswd -nb admin admin@123
admin:$apr1$JsindKAS$zCWAvabJOgQvI.Dd3zjtE.

You copy this value to the Traefik dynamic configuration (see Listing 2-17).

Listing 2-17. Basic auth middleware configuration in dynamic configuration file

```
# Dynamic configuration
http:
  routers:
    router0:
      entryPoints:
      - web
      middlewares:
      - basic-auth
      service: hello-world
      rule: Path(`/hello-world`)

  services:
    hello-world:
      loadBalancer:
        servers:
        - url: "http://localhost:9080/"

# Declaring the basic auth middleware with the user credentials
  middlewares:
    basic-auth:
      basicAuth:
        users:
          - "admin:$apr1$JsindKAS$zCWAvabJOgQvI.Dd3zjtE."
```

Now let's try the /hello-world endpoint in the browser. You get a basic auth prompt in the browser where you are asked to enter the username and password (see Figure 2-25). After entering these, you can see the response of the hello-world service (see Figure 2-26).

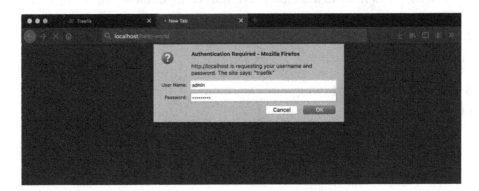

Figure 2-25. *Browser basic authentication*

Figure 2-26. *Final authenticated Hello World*

Let's try the same with curl on the command line (see Listing 2-18).

Listing 2-18. Testing basic auth middleware applied on localhost endpoint

```
→ traefik-config> curl localhost/hello-world
401 Unauthorized
→ traefik-config> curl -u admin localhost/hello-world
Enter host password for user 'admin':
Hello, World
```

Now that this is working, let's take one final look at the configuration in the Traefik dashboard. You see that the HTTP Middlewares tile on the main page now shows another middleware in the count (see Figure 2-27).

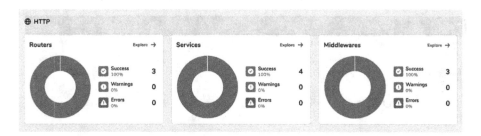

***Figure 2-27.** Final configuration*

You drill down to the Middlewares page where you can view the defined `basic-auth@file` middleware. Traefik automatically assigns the name. You also see other implicit middleware (see Figure 2-28).

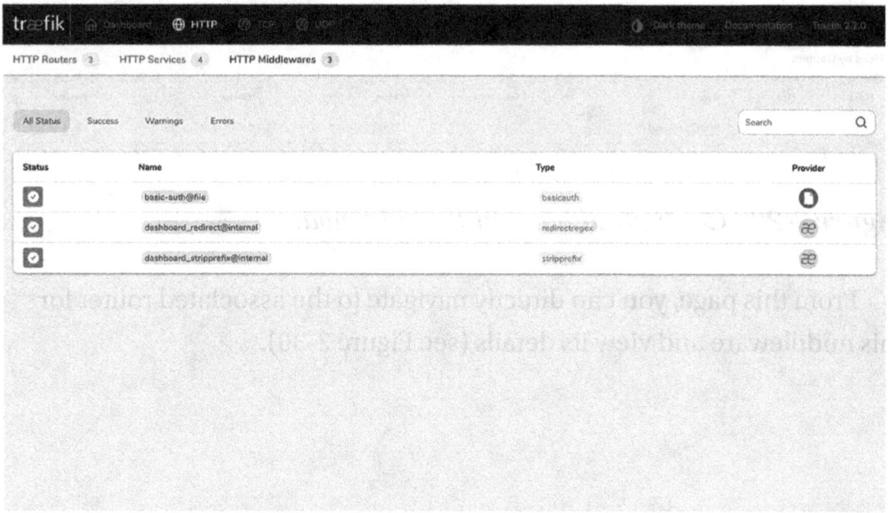

***Figure 2-28.** Drill down to configured HTTP middleware*

You then drill down further and view the configuration for the middleware. You can also see the user you defined for authentication (see Figure 2-29).

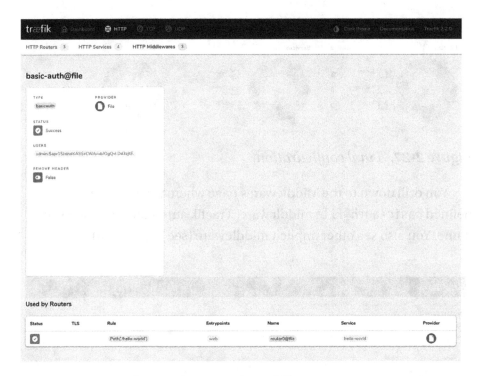

Figure 2-29. *Configured basic auth middleware*

From this page, you can directly navigate to the associated router for this middleware and view its details (see Figure 2-30).

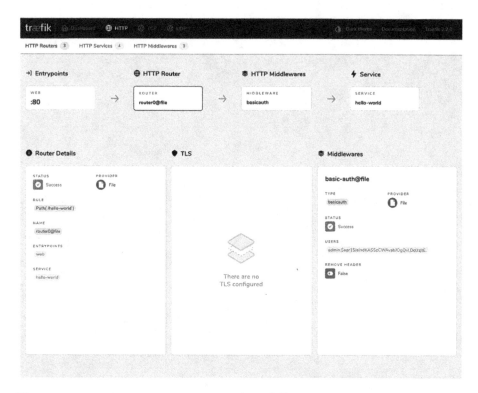

Figure 2-30. *Routers, services, and middleware connected*

Summary

In this chapter, you looked at basic configuration pieces of Traefik and how to manually configure Traefik to expose an API on a particular port and route traffic to the corresponding backend service. You looked at various ways to configure Traefik and passed configuration from a file, CLI parameters, and environment variables. You also did a deep dive into the Traefik dashboard to understand how to work with it to understand the configuration.

Until now, you have simply been routing traffic to one instance of a backing service. In the next chapter you deep dive into the load balancer capabilities of Traefik, for HTTP as well as TCP traffic.

CHAPTER 3

Load Balancing

Scaling is an important tenet of application design. Scaling not only provides application performance, but, if done right, scaling also provides application availability and fault tolerance. Developers must pay attention to effectively scaling the application. It can't be a post-development thought. Previously, you learned that an application can be scaled vertically by allocating more resources to a running instance. Monolithic applications follow this principle. Chapter 1 explained how this is an ineffective approach.

Moreover, to provide availability, we often pick a hot-cold deployment pattern. This drives inefficiency because a cold instance is a standby instance. It is only activated when the primary application instance is down.

On the other hand, horizontal scaling allows you to run more than one instance of the application simultaneously. Each of these instances can run on the minimum required hardware and serve user requests. It is the preferred mechanism for deploying an application in cloud environments. It greatly improves application availability by using hot-hot deployments (see Figure 3-1).

© Rahul Sharma, Akshay Mathur 2021
R. Sharma and A. Mathur, *Traefik API Gateway for Microservices*,
https://doi.org/10.1007/978-1-4842-6376-1_3

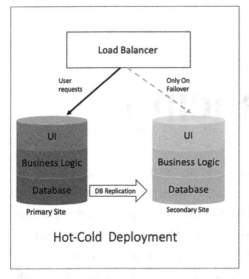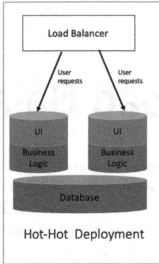

Figure 3-1. *Deployment types*

Once there are multiple instances of an application, a load balancer must be configured to work with them effectively. A load balancer application like Traefik can run at Layer 4 and Layer 7 of the open systems interconnection (OSI) model. At Layer 4, it serves as a TCP/UDP proxy. It works on the base of host and port information. At Layer 7, the load balancer looks at many attributes (e.g., HTTP load balancing can be done based on host, port, request path, or request headers). Thus, Traefik can perform load balancing at both layers.

In Chapter 2, we configured HTTP services in Traefik. In this chapter, we configure load balancing of HTTP services. Traefik also provides TCP and UDP capabilities. We work with them, as well.

HTTP Load Balancer

To effectively use horizontal scaling, we need a load balancer. The load balancer is configured with all instances of the application. When the load balancer receives a request, it must delegate the request to one of the configured instances. Several load balancing algorithms can alter the behavior of request handling. Each algorithm has pros and cons and works better for some situations than others.

In the previous chapter, we configured Traefik using file type provider. We created an entrypoint for port 80. We also added `routers` and `services` to handle incoming requests. The services configuration points to the location of an application. The load balancing algorithm is also governed at the service level. Several services can use a particular algorithm, while others can use a different algorithm. When we look at the service configuration, it consists of the following blocks.

- **Service**: Defines the logical grouping of servers so that common attributes can be applied

- **Server**: Defines the actual location of the application

Either of the two blocks configures load balancing in Traefik. In the following section, we configure the different attributes to learn complete behavior.

Round Robin

A round robin (RR) is one of the simplest algorithms for load distribution. The algorithm delegates requests to each available instance in equal proportions (see Figure 3-2). It performs the operation in a circular manner without any notion of priority or preference. Round-robin load balancing works best when servers have roughly identical computing capabilities.

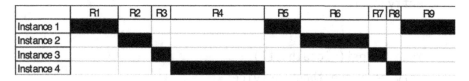

	R1	R2	R3	R4	R5	R6	R7	R8	R9
Instance 1	■				■				■
Instance 2		■				■			
Instance 3			■				■		
Instance 4				■				■	

Figure 3-2. *Request distribution*

In Figure 3-2, there are four servers in the application. The graph depicts how the algorithm distributes incoming requests among them. Going further, we need an HTTP application for configuring the round robin. In the remaining sections, we work with a visitor log-keeping application. The application has the following behaviors.

- Adds a guest name

- Lists the latest guest name

- Shows all guest names

The application is deployed on multiple boxes. Each application instance is given a name, which is shown in the UI (see Figure 3-3). The UI helps determine which instance serves the user request.

GuestBook Details- 9191

Create a New Guest Book Entry
Name

Figure 3-3. *Visitor log screen*

Traefik services configuration consists of a `service` and a `server` block. The round robin is configured by using a `server` block.

```
http :
  routers :
    guest-router :
      entryPoints :
      - web

      rule : Host(`localhost`)
      service : guestbook-service
```

```
services :
  guestbook-service :
    loadBalancer :
      servers :
        - url   : "http://192.168.1.10:9090/"
        - url   : "http://192.168.1.11:9191/"
```

The following is configured in the preceding code.

- Request routing is configured for the `localhost` domain. The rule matches all incoming requests. In the previous chapter, you saw the PATH rule, which validates request URL location. Here we are validating requests based on the hostname instead of the request path. Traefik uses the `guestbook-service` configuration to handle the request.

- The `server` section lists the URLs of all available instances. It is configured as a list of values.

Let's run the Traefik configuration and access http://localhost (see Figure 3-4) in the browser. Service configuration is also available on the Traefik dashboard (see Figure 3-5). It shows the complete status of a service.

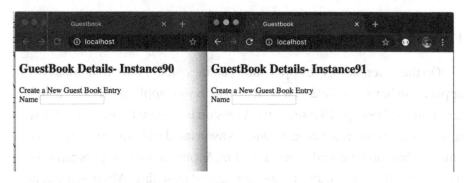

Figure 3-4. *Multiple instances of visitor*

If you refresh the browser a couple of times, you see that it is served from both instances. We can add a few entries to the application. This data is saved in the underlying database. The data is subsequently shown in both instances. In a nutshell, the application is not keeping any state. All states are persisted in the database. The classic round-robin algorithm is good enough when the complete application is stateless, like a visitor logbook.

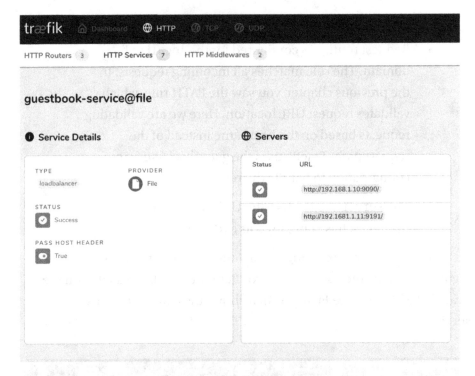

Figure 3-5. *Traefik dashboard for round robin*

On the other hand, the application can be stateful. This means each application has some data that is local to it. In web applications, the state is maintained using HTTP sessions. A session is created for every user. The session is an in-memory store. It remains associated with the user. There is no limit to what can be stored inside a session. Application developers can store user-centric data like id, latest transactions, and UI styling. When requests are routed from one instance to another, the session information is lost.

Sticky Session

Session stickiness ensures that all requests from the user during the session are sent to the same instance. The load balancer implements this by persisting cookies in the user request. The load balancer creates a cookie for the first user request. It then refers to that cookie for every subsequent request. In Traefik, the cookie is configured at the loadBalancer level.

```
# Removed for Brevity

  services :
    guestbook-service :
      loadBalancer :
        sticky :
          cookie : {}
        servers :
        - url   : "http://192.168.1.10:9090/"
        - url   : "http://192.168.1.9:9191/"
```

In the code, we added the sticky attribute for a defined guest-service loadBalancer. After the change, the requests can no longer toggle between the two application instances. It is served from only one instance. We can validate the instance details by looking-up cookie details in the browser (see Figure 3-6).

Name	Value	Domain	Path	Expires / Max-A...	S...	HttpOnly	Secure	SameSite	Priority
_ca2c6	http://192.168.1.9:91...	localhost	/	Session	30				Medium

Figure 3-6. *Browser cookie*

The configuration added a cookie with a generated name. The `sticky` record provides the following optional attributes which can configure the behavior of the generated cookie.

- Name: Specifies a cookie name instead of a generated one.

- HttpOnly: The flag mitigates cookie access through client-side JavaScript.

- Secure: The attribute sends a cookie over an HTTPS connection.

- SameSite: The attribute restricts cookies within the same-site context. The context boundary is defined by the various values of the attribute.

The Traefik dashboard also shows the updated configuration (see Figure 3-7).

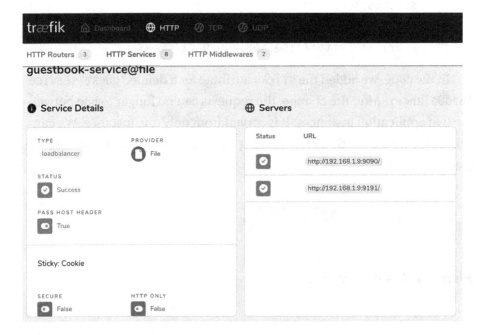

Figure 3-7. *Traefik dashboard for sticky session*

A cookie points to the server location that handled the original request. Traefik must be configured to monitor all these application servers. If the server specified in the cookie becomes unavailable, the request is forwarded to a new server. Traefik updates the cookie with details of the new server. This is achieved by configuring health checks for the instances.

Note   When using classic round robin routing Traefik keeps the unhealthy server until application health checks are configured.

Health Check

To work effectively, a load balancer should determine which backend servers are performing well. This is accomplished by sending requests to validate the instance status at periodic intervals. These requests are known as *health checks*. Traefik routes requests only to healthy instances. It keeps track of all active instances. Traefik drops an instance from the active instances pool when it determines the instance is unhealthy. It keeps monitoring unhealthy instances. Once the instance is restored, Traefik adds it back to the active instance pool. Only a response to the heath check request governs their status of the instance. Responses other than 2XX and 3XX are considered errors (see Figure 3-8).

```
HTTP ERROR 500

Problem accessing /. Reason:

    Server Error

Caused by:

javax.servlet.ServletException: org.springframework.web.util.NestedServletException: Request processing failed; nested exception is java.lang.RuntimeException: Application Error
    at org.eclipse.jetty.server.handler.HandlerCollection.handle(HandlerCollection.java:146)
    at org.eclipse.jetty.server.handler.HandlerWrapper.handle(HandlerWrapper.java:132)
    at org.eclipse.jetty.server.Server.handle(Server.java:502)
    at org.eclipse.jetty.server.HttpChannel.handle(HttpChannel.java:370)
    at org.eclipse.jetty.server.HttpConnection.onFillable(HttpConnection.java:267)
    at org.eclipse.jetty.io.AbstractConnection$ReadCallback.succeeded(AbstractConnection.java:305)
    at org.eclipse.jetty.io.FillInterest.fillable(FillInterest.java:103)
    at org.eclipse.jetty.io.ChannelEndPoint$2.run(ChannelEndPoint.java:117)
    at org.eclipse.jetty.util.thread.strategy.EatWhatYouKill.runTask(EatWhatYouKill.java:333)
    at org.eclipse.jetty.util.thread.strategy.EatWhatYouKill.doProduce(EatWhatYouKill.java:310)
    at org.eclipse.jetty.util.thread.strategy.EatWhatYouKill.tryProduce(EatWhatYouKill.java:168)
    at org.eclipse.jetty.util.thread.strategy.EatWhatYouKill.run(EatWhatYouKill.java:126)
    at org.eclipse.jetty.util.thread.ReservedThreadExecutor$ReservedThread.run(ReservedThreadExecutor.java:366)
    at org.eclipse.jetty.util.thread.QueuedThreadPool.runJob(QueuedThreadPool.java:765)
    at org.eclipse.jetty.util.thread.QueuedThreadPool$2.run(QueuedThreadPool.java:683)
    at java.lang.Thread.run(Thread.java:748)
```

Figure 3-8. *Application errors*

Traefik allows you to configure the server health using the health check attribute of the service.

```
services :
  guestbook-service :
      servers :
      - url   : "http://192.168.1.10:9090/"
      - url   : "http://192.168.1.11:9191/"
      healthCheck:
        path: /
        interval: "10s"
        timeout: "1s"
```

The following can be said about the preceding code.

- The / path is configured for health status lookup.

- The lookup is performed every 10 seconds. If the server changes its state, it is known after a maximum of 10 seconds.

- Timeout configures the time interval for HTTP request-timeout

To test the configuration, you can either stop one of the servers or raise an error response (5XX,4XX) from the application. These health checks are also visible in the Traefik dashboard under the Services tab. (see Figure 3-9)

Figure 3-9. *Traefik dashboard with application health*

When working with sticky sessions, Traefik resets the cookie if the server becomes unable. The request is then routed to one of the healthy servers. Traefik updates the cookie with details of the new instance. All further requests are routed to the new server.

Weighted Round Robin

The weighted round robin (WRR) considers the resource capacities of the application instances (see Figure 3-10). An instance with higher hardware specifications than others can handle more requests. This is done by assigning a weight to each instance. There are no specific criteria to determine the weight. This is left to the system administrator. The node with the higher specs is apportioned a greater number of requests. The diagram in Figure 3-10 shows the request distribution for WRR.

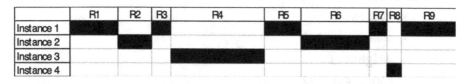

Figure 3-10. *Weighted distribution of requests*

So far, you learned that weights are assigned to a different instance of the application. But in Traefik, this is denoted at the service level rather than the server level. In a previous section, we configured the loadbalancer type of service. The service had the location of each of the servers. But to work with WRR, we need to divide servers logically into different load capacities. Each of these capacity service instances are grouped into a weighted service instance with the associated weights (see Figure 3-11).

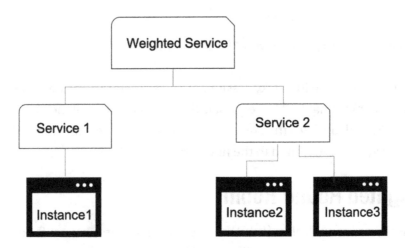

Figure 3-11. *Weighted service hierarchy*

```
# Removed for Brevity

    services :
     guestbook-service :
       weighted:
         services:
          - name: guestv1
            weight: 3
          - name: guestv2
            weight: 1
```

```
guestv1 :
  loadBalancer :
    servers :
    - url  : "http://192.168.1.10:9090/"  -- host 1
    - url  : "http://192.168.1.11:9191/"  -- host 2
guestv2 :
  loadBalancer :
    servers :
    - url  : "http://192.168.1.12:9292/"  -- Host 3
```

The following can be said about the preceding code.

- There are three hosts for above application. Host1 and Host2 are grouped together.

- guestv1 defined configuration of grouped hosts. guestv2 defined configuration for host three instance.

- guestbook-service configures both logical groups in ratio 3:1. Traefik sends every fourth request to h3 while the remaining requests are distributed in a round-robin manner within host2 and host3.

You can see the weighted distribution in the Traefik dashboard shown in Figure 3-12.

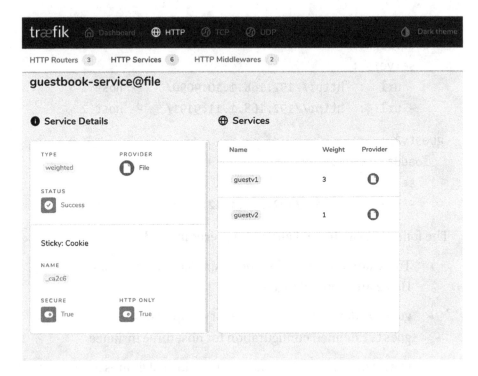

Figure 3-12. *Weighted service*

There is no health check for the weighted service. The health of the weighted service depends on the health configured for the underlying services.

Sticky Session

In the previous section, we enabled a sticky session to bind the user to a server. But when working with weighted services adding a sticky attribute to the `loadbalancer` service is not good enough. The weight service cannot recognize instance details from the cookie. To do so, we have to configure a cookie at the `weighted` service level. In summary, session stickiness is maintained at all levels of the service hierarchy. Thus, we need to add a cookie at the weighted service level and the load balancer level.

```
services :
  guestbook-service :
    weighted:
      services:
      - name: guestv1
        weight: 3
      - name: guestv2
        weight: 1
      sticky:
        cookie:
          httpOnly: true

  guestv1 :
    loadBalancer :
      sticky:
        cookie:
          httpOnly: true
      servers :
      - url   : "http://192.168.1.10:9090/"
      - url   : "http://192.168.1.9:9191/"

  guestv2 :
    loadBalancer :
      servers :
      - url   : "http://192.168.1.11:9292/"
```

The following can be said about the preceding code.

- It enables session stickiness for guestbook-service by adding the sticky attribute.

- It enables session stickiness for guestbookv1 by adding the sticky attribute.

The configuration added a cookie with a generated name. The `sticky` record has the optional attributes that can configure the behavior of the generated cookies. We can validate the attributes in Browser cookie console (see Figure 3-13). The configured cookie details are also visible on Traefik dashboard (see Figure 3-14).

Name	Value	Domain	Path	Expires / Max-A...	S...	HttpOnly	Secure	SameSite	Priority
_2f3d7	guestv2	localhost	/	Session	13	✓			Medium
_ca2c6	http://192.168.1.9:91...	localhost	/	Session	30				Medium

Figure 3-13. *Browser cookies for all services*

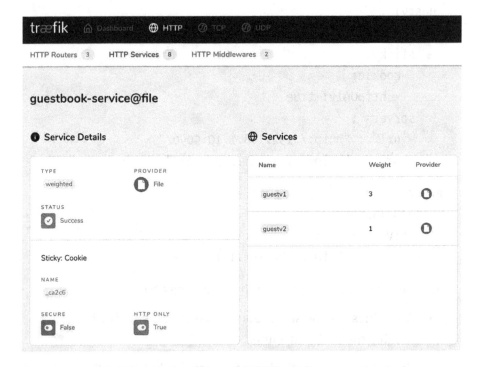

Figure 3-14. *Sticky session for weighted service*

Note   Traefik also supports dynamic request routing where weights are evaluated for every request. But the feature is available in 1.X and not in 2.X.

Mirroring

Traffic shadowing or Mirroring is a deployment pattern where production traffic is copied and sent to two places. The original production server gets the actual request and the same get duplicated to a test environment. This process helps validate regression issues in the new version of the application. If the testing version has the same request URLs and parameters, then mirroring can validate if the new version is as close to bug-free as possible.

Traffic mirroring is often done asynchronously. This makes sure that the original request processing is not impacted in any manner. Moreover, all mirrored requests are fire and forget. In summary, the response from the mirror is ignored. It is not propagated back to the client in any scenario.

As a practice, we do not duplicate all requests to the mirror service. If done so, it would require a testing infrastructure that is comparable to production. Thus, only a percentage of the requests are replicated to the mirror service. Traefik configures a mirror service as a different type of service. It does not limit you to have one mirror service. We can add as many mirror services as we required. We are only required to create a hierarchy of services as it was done in WRR.

```
services :
    guestbook-service :
      mirroring:
        service: guestv1
        mirrors:
        - name: guestv2
          percent: 10
```

```
guestv1 :
  loadBalancer :
   sticky:
     cookie:
   servers :
   - url   : "http://localhost:9090/"
   healthCheck:
     scheme : http
     path: /
     interval: "10s"
     timeout: "1s"

guestv2 :
  loadBalancer :
    servers :
    - url   : "http://localhost:9191/"
    healthCheck:
      scheme : http
      path: /
      interval: "10s"
      timeout: "1s"
```

In the code, we did the following to create a mirror for guest-service.

- The top-level service (guest-service) is defined as a composite service consisting of two different services.

- The mirroring attribute tells that the current service is a mirroring service. We added only one mirror service.

- guestv2 is described as the mirror. It receives only 10 percent of the original request.

- Next, we define two loadBalancer services.

Lastly, we added healthCheck for each application. But the service derives its health from the underlying original production service(s). The health of the mirror has no impact on the heath of the original service. The configured mirror service is also show on the service view of Traefik dashboard (see Figure 3-15).

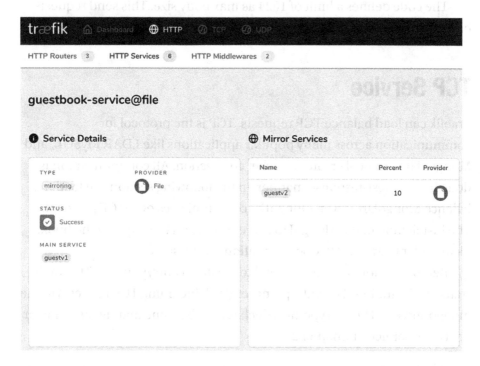

Figure 3-15. *Mirror service*

Besides sending a subset of requests, we often do not want to send large requests. Again, here as well, the limit is based on the infrastructure available with the mirror. This is done by setting up the maxBodySize attribute.

```
services :
  guestbook-service :
    mirroring:
      service: guestv1
      maxBodySize : 1024
```

85

```
    mirrors:
    - name: guestv2
        percent: 10

# Removed for brevity
```

The code defines a limit of 1024 as max body size. This send requests have a size less than 1024 for a mirror service.

TCP Service

Traefik can load balance TCP requests. TCP is the protocol for communication across many popular applications like LDAP, MySQL, and Mongo. The protocol creates a socket connection. All communication is done in a request-response manner. In the following section, we load the balance MongoDB server. MongoDB communicates over TCP protocol. The installation of the MongoDB server is beyond the scope of the book. Please refer to MongoDB documentation for the same.

Before we move ahead, we need to create an entrypoint for TCP in the static configuration. The entrypoint sends all incoming TCP requests to the mongo servers. The entrypoint is declared in the same manner as done for the HTTP service in Chapter 2.

```
entryPoints :
  mongo :
    address : ":80"

providers :
  file :
    directory : /Users/rahulsharma/traefik/ch03/code
    watch : true
    filename : config
```

```
api :
  insecure : true
  dashboard : true
```

Round Robin

We discussed the round-robin algorithm in the previous section. The algorithm distributes requests equally among the listed servers. Traefik allows you to load balance TCP services using the round-robin algorithm. As a prerequisite, you need to have MongoDB running on two servers.

```
tcp :
  routers :
    mongo-router :
      entryPoints :

      - mongo
      rule : HostSNI(`*`)
      service : mongo-tcp-service

  services :
    mongo-tcp-service:
      loadBalancer :
        servers :
        - address   : "192.168.1.10:27017"
        - address   : "192.168.1.11:27017"
```

The following can be said about the preceding code.

- It describes a mongo-router for routing requests to mongo-tcp-service.

- The TCP router has a single HostSNI rule. This enables you to operate a TCP and HTTP service on the same port. You see it when TLS support is enabled.

- `mongo-tcp-service` has the same declaration as an HTTP service. It consists of a `loadBalancer` block.

- The `loadBalancer` block contains a list of addresses, unlike the HTTP service, where the location was a URL. In TCP, this is a combination of an IP and a port.

The configured TCP services are shown in TCP service view of Traefik dashboard (see Figure 3-16).

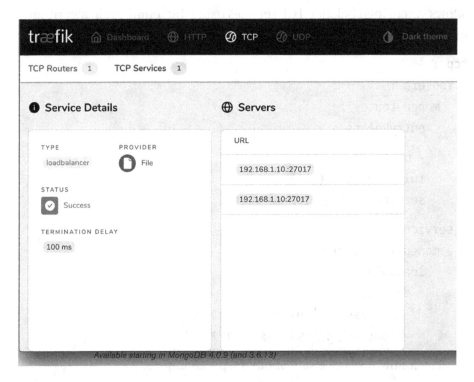

Figure 3-16. *Round-robin TCP service*

The following command connects to Mongo servers using the Mongo shell. You can determine which server is connected using the `db.hostInfo` command.

```
$traefik:/# mongo -u root -p example --host localhost --port 80
MongoDB shell version v4.2.6
connecting to: mongodb://
localhost:80/?compressors=disabled&gssapiServiceName=mongodb
Implicit session: session { "id" : UUID("6cc39569-0bc3-4602-
b582-566afaac0382") }
MongoDB server version: 4.2.6
Server has startup warnings:
2020-05-23T13:41:25.742+0000 I  STORAGE  [initandlisten]
2020-05-23T13:41:25.742+0000 I  STORAGE  [initandlisten] **
WARNING: Using the XFS filesystem is strongly recommended with
the WiredTiger storage engine
2020-05-23T13:41:25.742+0000 I  STORAGE  [initandlisten]
**        See http://dochub.mongodb.org/core/prodnotes-filesystem
---
>  db.hostInfo()
```

Terminal Delay

A TCP client makes a connection only once. It then sends all requests over the open connection. This is opposite to an HTTP protocol, where every request is routed on a new connection. But this presents another challenge. A connection can be closed from either side. It can be closed from the server due to various reasons like business validations and service restart. It can be closed from the client as well. Since TCP works in duplex mode, every connection closed event must be acknowledged from both sides. If the other end does not handle the connection closer, the connection stays half-open. The open connection would lock Traefik resources.

Connection close handling can be improved by configuring a termination delay. The delay defines a timeout interval during which Traefik waits for connection close from both sides. After the delay, Traefik terminates the connection and recollects the allocated resources. The delay clock is set when either party sends a close event.

```
# removed for Brevity

services :
    mongo-tcp-service:
      terminationDelay: 50
      loadBalancer :
        servers :
        - address   : "192.168.1.10:27017"
        - address   : "192.168.1.11:27017"
```

The delay is configured at the service level. It applies to all servers under the service. The delay has a positive value specifying the interval in milliseconds. A negative value indicates that the connection is held until it is closed by both parties.

Note   There are no status codes or equivalent in TCP protocol. Thus there is no health check available for TCP services.

Weighted Round Robin

In the previous section, we discussed the weighted round-robin algorithm. The algorithm allows you to distribute incoming TCP requests based on a prescribed weight ratio. As seen in the HTTP service example, the weighted service is a higher-order service than the loadBalancer service. It has the same behavior for TCP services as well. Continuing with the MongoDB servers from the last section, let's look at the weighted configuration.

```
# Removed for Brevity

  services :
    mongo-tcp-service :
      weighted:
        services:
          - name: mongo-1-service
            weight: 3
          - name: mongo-2-service
            weight: 1

    mongo-1-service:
      terminationDelay: 42
      loadBalancer :
        servers :
        - address   : "192.168.1.10:27017"
        - address   : "192.168.1.11:27017"

    mongo-2-service:
      terminationDelay: 42
      loadBalancer :
        servers :
        - address   : "192.168.1.12:27017"
```

The following can be said about the preceding code.

- There are three hosts for above application.
  192.168.1.10 and 192.168.1.11 are grouped together.

- mongo-1-service defined configuration of grouped
  hosts. mongo-2-service defined configuration for the
  host3 instance.

- Mongo-tcp-service configures both logical groups
  in ratio 3:1. Traefik sends every fourth connection
  request to 192.168.1.12 while the remaining requests
  are distributed in a round-robin manner within
  192.168.1.10 and 192.168.1.11.

We can see the weighted distribution in the Traefik dashboard. (see
Figure 3-17)

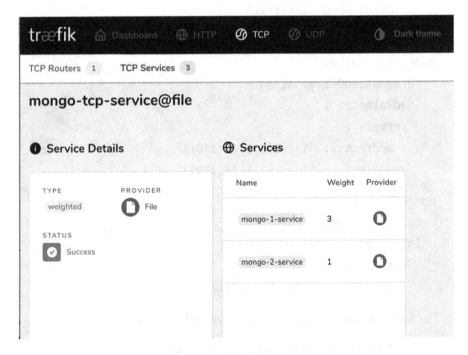

Figure 3-17. *Weighted round-robin TCP service*

UDP Service

Traefik can load balance UDP requests. UDP is the protocol for
communication across many popular applications like IMAP, DNS, TFTP,
and Memcache. UDP uses a connectionless communication model with
a minimum of protocol mechanism. There are no handshakes, and there

is no guaranteed delivery. Thus, the protocol has no overhead costs. Some applications require these attributes, like time-sensitive applications.

In the following section, we load balance TFTP servers. TFTP communicates over UDP protocol. The installation of a TFTP server is beyond the scope of this book. Please refer to TFTP/Unix documentation for more information.

Before we move ahead, we need to create an entrypoint, for UDP, in the static configuration. The entrypoint sends all incoming UDP traffic to the TFTP servers. The entrypoint declares in the same manner as for HTTP in Chapter 2.

```
entryPoints :
  tftp :
    address : ":69/udp"

providers :
  file :
    directory : /Users/rahulsharma/Projects/traefik-book/ch03/code
    watch : true
    filename : config

api :
  insecure : true
  dashboard : true
```

Round Robin

We discussed the round-robin algorithm in previous sections. The algorithm distributes requests equally among the listed servers. Traefik allows you to load balance UDP services using the round-robin algorithm. As a prerequisite, you need to have TFTP running on two servers.

```
udp :
  routers :
    tftp-router :
      entryPoints :
      - tftp
      service : tftp-service

  services:
    tftp-service:
      loadBalancer :
        servers :
        - address  : "192.168.1.10:69"
        - address  : "192.168.1.11:69"
```

The following can be said about the preceding code.

- We described tftp-router to route requests to tftp-service.

- A UDP router does not have any rules. It cannot perform hostname lookup. It can only be performed using a port.

- tftp-service has the same declaration as an HTTP service. It consists of a loadBalancer block.

- The loadBalancer block contains a list of addresses, unlike the HTTP service, where the location was a URL. In UDP, it is a combination of the IP and a port.

Traefik dashboard also provides a UDP service view to show the configured UDP services. (see Figure 3-18)

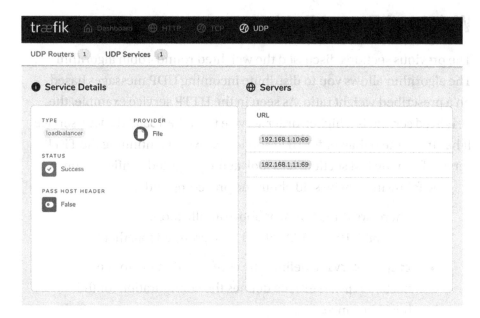

Figure 3-18. *UDP service in round robin*

Note   There is no health check available for UDP services.

The following command connects to TFTP servers by using the `tftp` command. You can transfer the sample files that we made available on the server.

```
traefik $ tftp 192.168.1.4
tftp> verbose
Verbose mode on.
tftp> get sample.md
getting from 192.168.1.4:sample.md to sample.md [netascii]
Received 682 bytes in 0.0 seconds [inf bits/sec]
```

Weighted Round Robin

The previous sections discussed the weighted round-robin algorithm. The algorithm allows you to distribute incoming UDP messages based on a prescribed weight ratio. As seen in the HTTP service example, the weighted service is a higher-order service than the loadBalancer service. It has the same behavior for UDP services as well. Continuing the TFTP servers from the last section, let's look at the weighted configuration.

The following can be said about the preceding code.

- There are three hosts for above application. 192.168.1.10 and 192.168.1.11 are grouped together.

- tftp-1-service defines the configuration of grouped hosts. tftp-2-service defines the configuration for the host3 instance.

- tftp-service configures both logical groups in ratio 3:1. Traefik sends every fourth connection request to 192.168.1.12 while the remaining requests are distributed in a round-robin manner within 192.168.1.10 and 192.168.1.11.

We can see the weighted distribution in the Traefik dashboard. (see Figure 3-19)

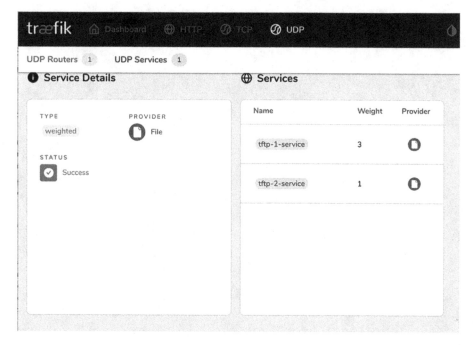

Figure 3-19. *Weighted UDP service*

Summary

In this chapter, you saw the different load balancing capabilities available in Traefik. We configured classic round robin and weighted round robin for HTTP, TCP, and UDP communication. You also worked with stick sessions and health checks for HTTP communication. Lastly, you saw mirroring capabilities that are used for canary deployments. In the next chapter, you look at TLS capabilities available in Traefik.

CHAPTER 4

Configure TLS

The previous chapters looked at how to expose services using Traefik over HTTP, TCP, and UDP connections. They also dove into the special traffic management features provided by Traefik. Until now, you have only worked with plain unencrypted traffic—HTTP or TCP. However, for any serious production usage, you need to expose the endpoints securely over TLS. In this chapter, you look at the capabilities that Traefik provides for encrypting and decrypting network traffic.

The following two scenarios are covered.

- TLS termination with Traefik
- TLS forwarding to backend services

For TLS termination at Traefik, we use Let's Encrypt to provision the TLS certificate automatically for a service running in a public cloud. Traefik and Let's Encrypt together make this complex process fairly trivial.

Quick Overview of TLS

The common use case of TLS encryption is to protect HTTP traffic. This means all API and web traffic is secured against man-in-the-middle attacks and other forms of network snooping. Instead of exposing plain HTTP traffic, we instead route the packets over HTTPS. This means the underlying channel over which the packets are transferred is encrypted.

© Rahul Sharma, Akshay Mathur 2021
R. Sharma and A. Mathur, *Traefik API Gateway for Microservices*,
https://doi.org/10.1007/978-1-4842-6376-1_4

A primary need for such security is to protect sensitive data, starting with username/password you may use to authenticate access to a protected resource. You should never transmit any secret over a plain HTTP connection as it can easily be intercepted by network sniffing software.

TLS traffic is encrypted when it leaves the source and is then decrypted at the destination end. The decryption part is what we refer to as *TLS termination*. This encryption and decryption are typically carried out much below the application layer (OSI or TCP/IP terms).

Most application layer code never needs to worry about the finer details of TLS, apart from specifying the appropriate configurations. Since implementing encryption protocols is not for the faint-hearted and should not be taken up lightly, most programming languages and platforms come with standard libraries that have been battle-tested and implemented by experts in cryptography.

Note   Although we are touching on many parts of working with TLS in Traefik, an in-depth discussion of TLS is beyond this book's scope. Its core is based on standard cryptographic primitives, specifically public-key cryptography, which is a specialized field. The walkthrough covers the practical aspects of working with TLS, which involve acquiring valid TLS certificates from a certificate authority and using them in the client-server configurations. We do not cover advanced network security practices or DNS, although we do brush past them. We encourage you to delve further into these areas to fine-tune configurations according to their use cases.

Broadly speaking, clients who connect to a server with TLS enabled can validate its authenticity. They do this by validating the server's TLS certificate with the certificate authority (or CA), which signed and issued the server's certificate. This server certificate contains the server's public key, which sets up an encrypted channel between the client and the server. This helps to guard against man-in-the-middle and other attacks. The CA is typically a trusted third-party public body, and most browsers already have these configured automatically. There is often a private CA for large private enterprise networks to issue certificates for internal Intranet sites, and this private CA is automatically trusted on the enterprise managed devices.

There is an extension to this mechanism to verify the client's identity to the server; this is achieved via client certificates typically issued by the same CA, validated on the server end. We are not covering this approach in this chapter, although Traefik has support for it.

Conventionally, the default port for HTTP traffic is 80, and HTTPS is 443, although various platforms and applications serve TCP and HTTP/HTTPS traffic on whatever ports they choose to. Ports 8080 and 8443, for instance, are very popular alternatives to expose HTTP and HTTPS traffic, respectively. (They are non-restricted ports, however that discussion is beyond the scope of this book.) Most Internet-facing servers, however, expose the standard ports 80 and 443. Until now, we have primarily exposed Traefik entrypoints on 8080, 80, or other custom ports for HTTP and TCP. The Traefik dashboard was exposed over HTTP 8080 or 80 in an insecure mode without authentication, which is not recommended for the production usage.

While TLS widely protects HTTP traffic on the web, we use it to secure plain TCP connections. We could easily expose HTTPS to one of the sample HTTP APIs covered in previous chapters. We feel TLS over simple TCP better exhibits the advanced TLS capabilities of Traefik. As part of exposing TCP ports over TLS, we also cover some HTTPS traffic.

TLS Termination at Traefik

The previous chapter covered how to use Traefik to expose and load balance a MongoDB TCP service. It is fine for local usage to have a plain connection; however, for any kind of serious production use case, you need to encrypt the connection to MongoDB using TLS. You can achieve this in two ways.

- Enable TLS on the MongoDB server, so TLS is terminated at the MongoDB server level. This requires Traefik to pass the encrypted traffic through. Or,

- MongoDB still serves plain TCP traffic; however, we enable TLS on the Traefik entrypoint to expose the MongoDB connection. TLS is then terminated at the Traefik entrypoint, which then passes the decrypted traffic to the backend MongoDB port.

Although the first option seems more favorable and secure, this is usually not a feasible approach in practice. Since Traefik typically acts as a load balancer or reverse proxy, it usually load balances your requests across multiple backend instances. This was covered in the last chapter.

Typically, you have multiple cluster nodes or service instances (for databases and APIs, respectively) being exposed behind a single route. In this scenario, any client expects a consistent endpoint to be exposed to whatever service they are connecting to. For security reasons, TLS certificates are closely coupled to the server domain host where they are deployed. If we did TLS termination at the individual instance level, then we need additional certificates or reuse the same certificate on each replica instance. To the consumer, it is apparent that the client is connecting to a different host each time. This is not very desirable.

In actual production, we always use Traefik for TLS termination and then route the packets from Traefik to the backend (MongoDB in the current example) over a simple TCP connection. This is not as big a security risk as it might seem because the internal traffic is in a closed network—typically your own VPC/VLAN. For scenarios with shared infrastructure, there is always the advanced practice of initiating a new internal TLS connection from your edge gateway to the backend service; we are not covering that.

Exposing MongoDB Route on TLS

This section runs a MongoDB instance on a cloud VM by a public cloud provider. You can use a managed database offering. You are free to use any other database if you adjust for the correct ports and use the appropriate client for that database. To keep things simple, we run both the MongoDB instance and Traefik on the same cloud VM so Traefik can securely connect to MongoDB running on the localhost without any other complexity.

For this example, we are running a single DigitalOcean droplet (or VM) running Ubuntu 18. However, the concepts are the same for any other cloud VM, such as an AWS EC2 instance. Setting up a DigitalOcean or AWS instance is beyond the scope of this book; however, it is easy to do. Once the VM is set up, Traefik can be easily installed using the instructions in Chapter 1.

Ubuntu Traefik CLI is not allowed to listen on ports 80 or 443 by default. So, Traefik throws an error on startup if those ports are defined as entrypoints. We need to run the command in Listing 4-1 to allow Traefik to bind to these ports.

Listing 4-1. Install and Set Permissions for Traefik

```
ubuntu-blr1-01:~$ wget https://github.com/containous/traefik/
releases/download/v2.2.1/traefik_v2.2.1_linux_amd64.tar.gz
ubuntu-blr1-01:~$ tar -zxvf traefik_v2.2.1_linux_amd64.tar.gz
ubuntu-blr1-01:~$ sudo setcap 'cap_net_bind_service=+ep' traefik
ubuntu-blr1-01:~$ ./traefik  --entryPoints.web.address=:80
```

You may wonder why we chose a cloud deployment. The reason is that we need a public DNS name for Traefik to acquire a valid TLS certificate. We set up a separate subdomain to point to the DigitalOcean droplet and added an A record in the DNS provider to point to its IP address (again, this discussion is beyond the scope of this book). You can try Traefik's TLS support locally, but you need manually provisioned or self-signed certificates. You would also miss how easy Traefik makes the entire process. The TLS configuration for manually acquired certificates is simple; we are providing it here for reference. This is the same for both valid public domain certificates and local self-signed test certificates.

Listing 4-2 defines a TCP route with a `tls: {}` key. This is enough to enable TLS on this route.

Listing 4-2. Route Configuration for MongoDB TCP over TLS: Manual Certificates

```
# traefik.yml with only 443 entrypoint
entryPoints:
  websecure:
    address: ":443"
# Also enable DEBUG log
log:
  level: DEBUG
providers:
  file:
```

```
    filename: "traefik-tls-conf.yml"
    watch: true
```

traefik-tls-conf.yml

```
tcp :
  routers :
    mongo-router :
      entryPoints :
      - websecure
      rule : "HostSNI(`localhost`) || HostSNI(`127.0.0.1`)"
      service : mongo-tcp-service
      tls: {} #This block will enable TLS for this route
#We also need to provide the TLS certificates
tls:
  certificates:
    - certFile: localhost+1.pem
      keyFile: localhost+1-key.pem
```

We also provide the certificate paths in a separate section. This is
a dynamic configuration, which means we can add new certificates at
runtime. These can only be defined via FileProvider. The correct certificate
is used at runtime based on the domain matched. If you don't provide
your own certificates, or don't provide one for a matching domain, Traefik
generates and uses its default self-signed certificate. It is possible to
override this default certificate as well. Manual certificate generation is
beyond the scope of this chapter. For local testing, a tool such as the one at
https://mkcert.dev/ can be useful. In the preceding configuration, you
can connect to MongoDB over a secure TCP+TLS connection.

Installation of MongoDB is outside the book; however, it is mostly
the default installation with one addition—we set up a DB user and
password for basic security. For simplicity, we use only a single backend
MongoDB instance, rather than load balancing across multiple ones. The
configuration looks like Listing 4-3.

Listing 4-3. Route Configuration for MongoDB TCP over TLS

```
#tls-config.yaml dynamic config
tcp :
  routers :
    mongo-router :
      entryPoints :
      - mongo
      rule : "HostSNI(`tlstraefik.rahulsharma.page`)"
      service : mongo-tcp-service
      tls:
        certResolver: "letsencrypt"
        domains:
          - main: "tlstraefik.rahulsharma.page"

  services :
    mongo-tcp-service :
      loadBalancer :
        servers :
        - address   : "localhost:27017"
```

Most of these pieces are already known to us. We looked at the HostSNI attribute. In previous examples, we set it to match all possible hostnames (*). While this approach may be fine for unencrypted traffic, it is not feasible with TLS. It matches the actual domain name where the services are running, and the server certificate validates the same. tlstraefik. rahulsharma.page is the public DNS name pointing to the IP address of the DigitalOcean droplet. There is also a certresolver attribute set to letsencrypt, which automates the provisioning of a TLS certificate from Let's Encrypt on the first request to this endpoint.

Let's Encrypt Automatic Certificate Provisioning

Acquiring TLS certificates is typically a multistep process. There are good utilities on all platforms which help you generate the necessary pieces. For how ubiquitous TLS certificates are, certificate generation is a complex procedure with many attributes to be set, and if some configuration is wrong, you need to start over. The usual steps are to generate a certificate signing request (CSR) for the server certificate and submit it to a CA for signing. The CA signs and returns a valid certificate that can be used. Different CAs have different pricing models, and certificate features and websites are free to pick and choose which ones they want to go with. This has traditionally been a manual process, with some automated parts.

The big disruption in this space was brought about by a non-profit called Let's Encrypt (`https://letsencrypt.org`). Let's Encrypt has issued free TLS certificates (over a billion of them) for over 225 million websites. It does this by automating the entire process via programmatic APIs, so no manual intervention is required.

Let's Encrypt ships several official and third-party clients, making the certificate provisioning process trivial for end users. It achieves this automation by leveraging the ACME standard (`https://tools.ietf.org/html/rfc8555`), which stands for Automatic Certificate Management Environment. We do not dive deeper into this, but it entirely automates the work of acquiring and managing certificates from an ACME-compliant CA. Mostly, all you must do is start up your HTTPS server, and the rest is taken care of. If someone is considering setting up a website that requires TLS certificates, Let's Encrypt is the way to go.

Note   Let's Encrypt only provisions certificates for public Internet-facing sites. This means your endpoints need to be reachable by a public domain name for Let's Encrypt to provision a TLS certificate. For private or internal APIs, certificates need to be provisioned from other CAs. This has an impact on the examples, which have been running on a local system so far.

Provisioning TLS Certificates for Public TCP Endpoints

To automatically provision a TLS certificate from Let's Encrypt, we need to expose the MongoDB port on the public Internet.

Obviously, you should never actually expose your database port on the Internet as a practice. There have been many news reports about unsecured MongoDB connections exposed on the open Internet and targeted by hackers, resulting in compromised data. We are using a blank DB for a short while for the example, so it should be fine. We are also protecting MongoDB with proper access credentials, and the port is only accessible through Traefik. One point to note here is that we also set up cloud firewall rules on a VM to only inbound traffic on ports 80, 443, and 4445. All other inbound traffic from the Internet is blocked.

As seen in Listing 4-2, we expose the Mongo TCP endpoint on the tlstraefik.rahulsharma.page domain. tlstraefik here is the subdomain on which the TLS route is matched. The certificate issued by Let's Encrypt is issued for the same subdomain. There is support for additional domain entries, which request additional SNI (Server Name Indication) hostnames that support multiple domains and TLS certificates on the same IP and port. We are not going to dive deeply into this.

Traefik first checks the domain entries and then the HostSNI value to figure out domains for which TLS certificates are automatically requested. Both are not needed here; we only included them for reference. This is more useful with wildcard certificates, which are not covered here.

The certresolver attribute is referenced. It is defined in the static configuration along with the entrypoint. We need to define a TLS entrypoint and the certificate resolvers, which is currently mostly Let's Encrypt.

In Listing 4-4, there are two items of interest. First is the caServer URL attribute to be specified. Ordinarily and by default, this is the Let's Encrypt production API endpoint. However, this endpoint has strict (though liberal) rate limits.

Listing 4-4. Entrypoint and Certificate Resolver

```
#traefik.yaml static config
entryPoints:
  mongo:
    address: ':4445'
  https:
    address: ':443'
providers:
  file:
    watch: true
    filename: tls-config.yml
certificatesResolvers:
  letsencrypt:
    # ACME support via Let's Encrypt
    acme:
      # Email address required for certificate registration
      email: "<email address>"
```

```
# File or key required for certificates storage.
storage: "acme.json"

# CA server URL
caServer: "https://acme-staging-v02.api.letsencrypt.org/
           directory"

tlsChallenge: {}
```

If you're new to Let's Encrypt and experimenting with configurations in a test environment to figure out your TLS settings, it makes more sense to use the URL of the Let's Encrypt staging endpoint, which is used in Listing 4-4. This does not provide a usable TLS certificate. The CA to sign the certificate is fake, and most browsers reject the resultant certificate. Let's Encrypt allows you to download the dummy CA certificate (fakelerootx1.pem) and validates your generated server certificate against it. This allows you to test out the overall integration before moving to production with a valid certificate.

Second, the `tlsChallenge` attribute is of interest. To validate that the third-party requesting a server certificate has ownership of the host machine, Let's Encrypt supports various automated challenges. The standard ones are the HTTP-01 challenge and the DNS-01 challenge. Both are suitable for different types of use cases. However, there is a special challenge for TLS terminating reverse proxies, which is the role Traefik is playing here, known as the TLS-ALPN-01 challenge. More information is beyond the scope of this book. This challenge type is trivial to configure in Traefik, so it is used here.

There is one caveat: this challenge requires Traefik to access port 443; hence, we exposed an additional entrypoint on port 443. This is not a big deal because we are using this port in the next section anyway. For a cloud-based installation, it is necessary to open port 443 in the inbound traffic firewall rules. When you check this out on the Traefik dashboard, you see two entrypoints (see Figure 4-1).

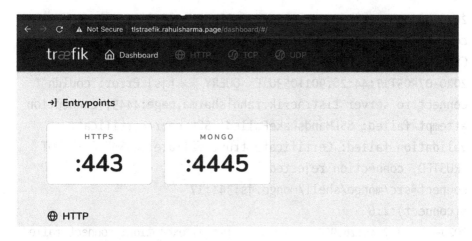

Figure 4-1. *TLS entrypoints*

If you use this Traefik configuration to expose a MongoDB instance running on the same server as the Traefik instance, you can access MongoDB on port 4445 on the hostname tlstraefik.rahulsharma.page, but only with a TLS connection. You can try this out with a Mongo client CLI (see Listing 4-5).

Listing 4-5. Mongo Client Simple Connection

```
ch04 % mongo --port 4445 --host tlstraefik.rahulsharma.page
MongoDB shell version v4.2.7
connecting to: mongodb:// tlstraefik.rahulsharma.page:4445/?com
pressors=disabled&gssapiServiceName=mongodb
```

This does not connect to the Mongo instance, and it does not work. To make it work, we need to pass a --tls option (see Listing 4-6).

Listing 4-6. Mongo Client TLS Connection

```
ch04 % mongo --port 4445 --host tlstraefik.rahulsharma.page --tls
MongoDB shell version v4.2.7
connecting to: mongodb:// tlstraefik.rahulsharma.page:4445/?com
pressors=disabled&gssapiServiceName=mongodb
```

111

```
2020-07-05T17:44:26.901+0530 E  NETWORK  [js] SSL peer
certificate validation failed: Certificate trust failure:
CSSMERR_TP_NOT_TRUSTED; connection rejected
2020-07-05T17:44:26.901+0530 E  QUERY    [js] Error: couldn't
connect to server tlstraefik.rahulsharma.page:4445, connection
attempt failed: SSLHandshakeFailed: SSL peer certificate
validation failed: Certificate trust failure: CSSMERR_TP_NOT_
TRUSTED; connection rejected :
connect@src/mongo/shell/mongo.js:341:17
@(connect):2:6
2020-07-05T17:44:26.904+0530 F  -    [main] exception: connect failed
2020-07-05T17:44:26.904+0530 E  -    [main] exiting with code 1
```

This does not work either; if you used the staging CA URL for
Let's Encrypt, the resultant server certificate cannot be verified. To connect
to MongoDB with this certificate, you need to either pass a –tlsAllowInvalid
Certificates flag or the --tlsCAFile option (see Listing 4-7).

Listing 4-7. Mongo Client TLS Connection

```
ch04 % mongo --port 4445 --host tlstraefik.rahulsharma.page -
tls --tlsCAFile fakelerootx1.pem
MongoDB shell version v4.2.7
connecting to: mongodb:// tlstraefik.rahulsharma.page:4445/?com
pressors=disabled&gssapiServiceName=mongodb
Implicit session: session { "id" : UUID("0b2ccc38-f8bd-4346-
a08a-3da0ef9793b0") }
MongoDB server version: 3.6.3
> use admin
switched to db admin
> db.auth("akshay", "password");
```

```
1
> db.version()
3.6.3
```

If you simply omit the caServer URL attribute in Listing 4-4, Traefik automatically connects to the Let's Encrypt production URL and fetches a valid certificate. Then, a command of the form seen in Listing 4-8 works.

Listing 4-8. Mongo Client Valid TLS Certificate

```
ch04 % mongo --port 4445 --host tlstraefik.rahulsharma.page –tls
MongoDB shell version v4.2.7
connecting to: mongodb:// tlstraefik.rahulsharma.page:4445/?com
pressors=disabled&gssapiServiceName=mongodb
Implicit session: session { "id" : UUID("0b2ccc38-f8bd-4346-
a08a-3da0ef9793b0") }
MongoDB server version: 3.6.3
>
```

There are two subtle points to note here. First, Traefik saves the acquired certificate in a file named acme.json by default. You saw this filename configured in Listing 4-4. We can add a custom file name or location if required. If you switch from staging to production URL, you also need to remove this file or use some other location; otherwise, Traefik uses the already saved certificate by default.

Second, while TLS termination may be tied closely to the entrypoint port (4445 in this case), TLS configuration is driven by the dynamic router configuration. What this boils down to is that Traefik does not send a certificate generation request to Let's Encrypt until it is configured for a particular route. Consequently, it is completely feasible for different certificates to be generated for the same entrypoint to serve different routes.

We can see the following TCP Router in the Traefik dashboard with the TLS details mentioned (see Figure 4-2 and Figure 4-3).

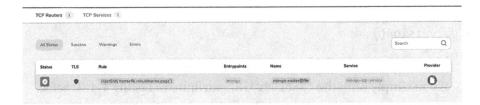

Figure 4-2. *TCP router with TLS enabled*

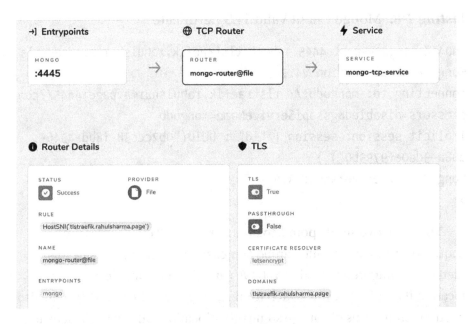

Figure 4-3. *TCP router with TLS details*

Secure Traefik Dashboard over TLS

Until now, we have exposed the Traefik dashboard in insecure mode to check the configurations on the UI. However, on a public cloud, you want the dashboard to be protected by authentication and TLS. As part of this, we expose the Traefik dashboard on entrypoint 443 on the same host and apply an authentication middleware on an explicit dashboard route. The route is exposed on the same hostname, although we could have specified a different hostname for the dashboard with its DNS entry and TLS certificate. The configuration for this is seen in Listing 4-9. We also redirect all HTTP traffic on port 80 to HTTPS on port 443.

Listing 4-9. Entrypoint and Route Config for Secure Dashboard

```
#traefik.yaml static config
entryPoints:
  https:
    address: ':443'
  http:
    address: :80
    http:
      redirections:
        entryPoint:
          to: https
          scheme: https
providers:
  file:
    watch: true
    filename: tls-config.yml
api:
  dashboard: true
#tls-config.yaml dynamic config
http:
  routers:
    dashboard:
      entryPoints:
        - https
      rule: "Host(`tlstraefik.rahulsharma.page`) &&
      (PathPrefix(`/api`) || PathPrefix(`/dashboard`))"
      service: api@internal
```

```
    tls:{}
    middlewares:
      - auth
middlewares:
  auth:
    basicAuth:
      users:
        - "admin:$apr1$JsindKAS$zCWAvabJOgQvI.Dd3zjtE."
```

On applying this configuration, you may observe two different results. If you already carried out the previous sections' steps to configure TLS for MongoDB, then Traefik reuses the server the same certificate acquired for the MongoDB route since they share the same host entry. However, if you omit the MongoDB TLS configuration, Traefik falls back to generating a default self-signed TLS certificate. You observe something like what's shown in Figure 4-4 in the browser, where it complains about the certificate and does not let you proceed. The reason for this is we have not specified any certResolver value for the dashboard route.

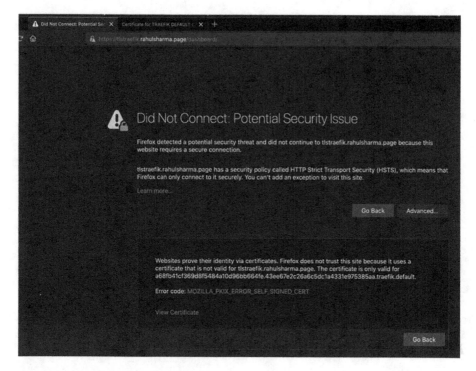

Figure 4-4. *Self-signed Traefik certificate error*

If we inspect the certificate, we get to see the details (see Figure 4-5).

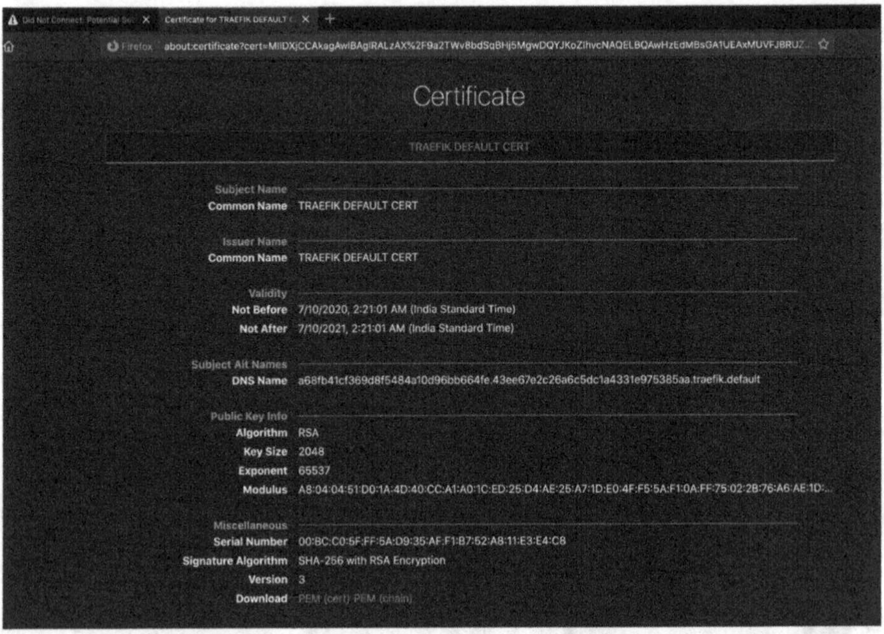

Figure 4-5. *Self-signed Traefik certificate details*

You can use a `certResolver` attribute for the dashboard route as well. You can even have two `certResolver` attributes within the configuration: one pointing to Let's Encrypt staging and one to production. An example of that is seen in Listing 4-10, where we define a different domain (it still must be a valid public domain) and a staging `certResolver` for the dashboard.

Listing 4-10. Multiple Lets Encrypt Resolvers

```
#traefik.yaml has both staging and prod LE config
# only relevant config for brevity
certificatesResolvers:
  letsencrypt:
    acme:
      email: "<email address>"
      storage: "acme.json"
```

```
      tlsChallenge: {}
  letsencrypt-staging:
    acme:
      email: "<email address>"
      storage: "acme-staging.json"
      # CA server to use.
      caServer: "https://acme-staging-v02.api.letsencrypt.org/
                  directory"
      tlsChallenge: {}
#tls-config.yaml dynamic config
http:
  routers:
    dashboard:
      entryPoints:
        - https
      rule: "Host(`dashboard.rahulsharma.page`) &&
      (PathPrefix(`/api`) || PathPrefix(`/dashboard`))"
      service: api@internal
      tls:
        certResolver: "letsencrypt-staging"
# Rest of config omitted for brevity
```

With this configuration, you see the following error in the browser (see Figure 4-6), and it does not allow you to proceed.

Figure 4-6. *Let's Encrypt staging certificate details*

Once we fix the configuration and get the proper production certificate from Let's Encrypt, we can inspect the certificate details in the browser (see Figure 4-7). We are also asked for the basic authentication credentials for the dashboard (see Figure 4-8).

Figure 4-7. *Let's Encrypt valid certificate details*

Figure 4-8. *Basic authentication for dashboard*

Traefik for TLS Forwarding

There may be certain rare occasions where your target service or database need to manage TLS termination on its own, without involving a reverse proxy in between. This means Traefik is required to forward TLS traffic without decrypting or terminating it. Happily, Traefik supports this easily via the passthrough option. We need to run MongoDB with server TLS

121

enabled and a valid TLS certificate to demonstrate this support. The configuration is outside the scope of this book; however, this should be easily doable by following the MongoDB documentation. The MongoDB configuration may end up looking, as shown in Listing 4-11.

Listing 4-11. Sample MongoDB TLS Configuration in /etc/mongod.conf

```
net:
  port: 27017
  bindIp: 127.0.0.1,tlstraefik.rahulsharma.page
   tls:
      mode: requireTLS
      certificateKeyFile: /etc/ssl/mongodb.pem
```

As before, you are free to choose any other target such as another cloud managed database, the procedure to connect is different. You can try this locally as well; you need self-signed server certificates and your own CA certificate. A deeper discussion of this is beyond the scope of this section; however, OpenSSL is a good utility available on all major platforms to generate TLS certificates.

This section's Traefik setup is the same Traefik instance as before running on the same cloud VM host with the necessary Traefik ports exposed on the firewall. However, this time instead of defining a certResolver for the mongo-router route, we add a different attribute, as shown in Listing 4-12.

Listing 4-12. Route Configuration for TLS Forwarding

#tls-config.yaml dynamic config
```
tcp :
  routers :
    mongo-router :
      entryPoints :
```

```
- mongo
  rule : "HostSNI(`tlstraefik.rahulsharma.page`)"
  service : mongo-tcp-service
  tls:
    passthrough: true
```

 # Rest omitted for brevity

When we try to access MongoDB on this host/port, Traefik forwards the TLS connection without decryption to the MongoDB server running on the same VM, where the actual TLS termination takes place, as shown in Listing 4-13.

Listing 4-13. Connect Mongo over TLS

```
code % mongo --tls --host tlstraefik.rahulsharma.page --port 4445
MongoDB shell version v4.2.8
connecting to: mongodb://tlstraefik.rahulsharma.page:4445/?comp
ressors=disabled&gssapiServiceName=mongodb
Implicit session: session { "id" : UUID("88df0a97-6ff8-4764-
897b-82746b621598") }
MongoDB server version: 4.2.8
> use admin
switched to db admin
> db.auth("akshay", "password");
1
```

If you inspect this configuration on the Traefik dashboard, you see the passthrough attribute set to true (see Figure 4-9).

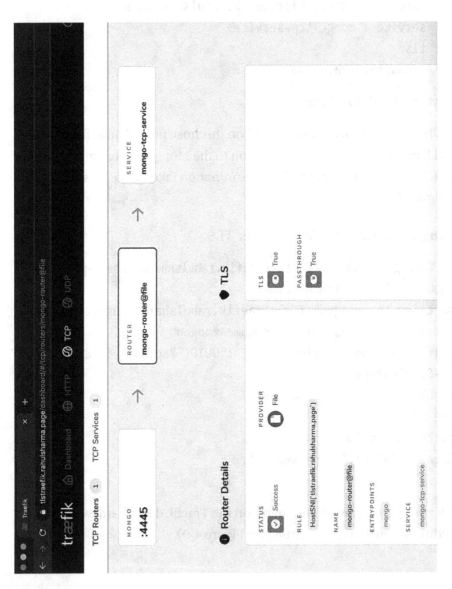

Figure 4-9. Traefik router with TLS passthrough

For the client application, there is no real change in behavior. With that, we wrap up this section and this chapter. For further deep dive, we encourage you to delve into the different TLS configuration options available in the Traefik documentation on their own.

Summary

In this chapter, you took a quick, surface-level dip into the deep domain of setting up TLS certificates to protect your network traffic. We understand that some of you may feel overwhelmed by all the subjects we rushed through. We have barely scratched the surface of the ecosystem of TLS certificates. However, we feel that we have exhibited how easy Traefik makes this in conjunction with Let's Encrypt, especially for a public DNS domain. Indeed, you may find that it is easier to provision a valid TLS certificate for Traefik endpoints from Let's Encrypt than it is to generate your self-signed or valid TLS certificates. If you are more interested in TLS, we encourage you to explore it.

We have not mentioned that certificates acquired through Let's Encrypt renew every 90 days for security. In the traditional IT landscape, certificate renewal is a tedious manual process that must be tracked by people. As a result, it is done less often with long-running TLS certificates being used. With the Traefik/Let's Encrypt integration, this is automatically handled out of the box without any manual intervention needed. Let's Encrypt will send out automatic advance reminders on the email address you registered with.

In the next chapter, you take a deeper look at the vast array of easy options available in Traefik for operational concerns. Traefik makes it very easy to gather runtime metrics and integrates out of the box with many standard monitoring frameworks.

CHAPTER 5

Logs, Request Tracing, and Metrics

Business operations perform application monitoring. This process aims to discover and fix application outages before they impact regular business operations. Traditionally, teams performed simple checks like process up/down or port open/closed. But these checks were not good enough. Over time, many tools have been built to improve the process of application monitoring. The process involves capturing usage metrics and performing analysis. But relying only on application monitoring is a weak practice. Application monitoring can only provide notifications on ongoing application issues. The next step is to determine the *root cause*.

The root cause is mostly contextual: a new feature is malfunctioning, or some controls were missed in the specification, or a user is executing a valid request that results in "out of memory," and so forth. We are unable to reach a conclusion by only looking at notifications. We need more information to determine the root cause. This is known as the *context-of-the-failure*.

Context is created by first looking at application logs, if available. A stack trace provides a lead into a possible bug, but the bug is caused by a particular edge scenario. These edge scenarios are defined by user data and the application state. User data is determined from request access logs if they have been captured. All of this is easier said than done.

© Rahul Sharma, Akshay Mathur 2021
R. Sharma and A. Mathur, *Traefik API Gateway for Microservices*,
https://doi.org/10.1007/978-1-4842-6376-1_5

Over the years, the enterprise application landscape has become more and more complex. Previous practices were insufficient in dealing with outages. Google came out with the practice of *request tracing*. Request tracing captured the flow of user requests across different distributed systems. This complementary process helped project failing scenarios and the systems involved.

In summary, logs, metrics, and traces are complementary practices (see Figure 5-1) for different purposes. None of these practices is individually sufficient during an outage. Thus, the simple practice of application monitoring has moved from the individual application state to a holistic view of the entire ecosystem. This is also known as *observability*. Observability encompasses gathering, visualization, and analysis of metrics, logs, and traces to gain a holistic understanding of a system's operation.

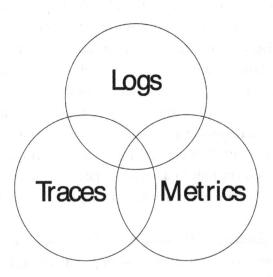

Figure 5-1. *Observability data*

Companies like Twitter, Google, Uber, and so forth, which pioneered observability, defined the complete practice built on the following pillars.

- Application and business metrics

- Logs

- Distributed traces

- Alerts and notifications

- Visualizations

Note   Observability projects why something is wrong, compared to monitoring, which simply tells when something is wrong.

Traefik, being the API-gateway, is a single point of entry of all externally originated user requests. It must integrate with enterprise existing solutions to capture all request flows and metrics. To capture end-to-end request flows, Traefik needs to generate request spans and send them the tracing backend system. Traefik also needs to generate access logs and request-based metrics to build visibility into distributed systems' behavior. This chapter discusses these features with a sample HTTP application.

Prerequisites

In this chapter, we use an example HTTP service. We deploy and configure the httpbin service (https://github.com/postmanlabs/httpbin) to serve our purposes. It is an open source application. The service is written in Python. We require a Python runtime to run the application. The deployed service is configured using Traefik.

Note   This is an optional step. It is an example service for validating configuration changes. If you have a running service, you can skip this step.

First, check for the required `python, pip,` and `virtualenv` commands.

```
~/Projects$ python3 --version
Python 3.8.0
```

```
~/Projects$ pip3 --version
pip 19.2.3 from /Library/Frameworks/Python.framework/
Versions/3.8/lib/python3.8/site-packages/pip (python 3.8)
```

```
~/Projects$ virtualenv --version
16.7.8
```

Make sure that you have the 3.x versions of Python and pip. If a command fails, you need to install the required software. Installation instructions for Python, pip, and virtualenv are beyond the scope of the book.

For the next step, we download a version of the httpbin service from release pages `https://github.com/postmanlabs/httpbin/releases` (see Figure 5-2). At the time of writing, 0.6.1 is the latest release version.

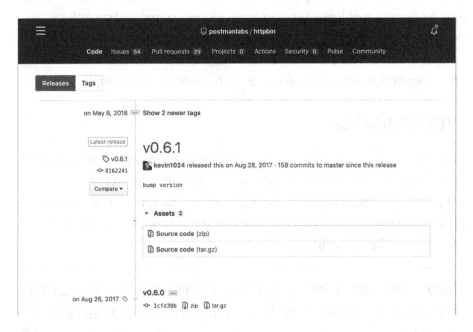

Figure 5-2. *httpbin releases*

Download the released artifacts and extract them to a directory. The directory contains the source files, application license, build files, and so forth. The aim is to compile the code and get a binary artifact from it.

```
~/Projects/httpbin-0.6.1$ ls -1
AUTHORS
Dockerfile
LICENSE
MANIFEST.in
Pipfile
Pipfile.lock
Procfile
README.md
app.json
build
dist
httpbin
httpbin.egg-info
setup.cfg
setup.py
test_httpbin.py
tox.ini
```

The service is built using setuptools. You can deploy and run the service, as explained next.

1. Create a virtual environment and then activate it.

```
~/Projects/httpbin-0.6.1$ virtualenv venv
Using base prefix '/Library/Frameworks/Python.framework/
Versions/3.8'
New python executable in /Users/rahulsharma/Projects/
httpbin-0.6.1/venv/bin/python3.8
```

```
Also creating executable in /Users/rahulsharma/Projects/
httpbin-0.6.1/venv/bin/python
Installing setuptools, pip, wheel...
done.
~/Projects/httpbin-0.6.1$ source venv/bin/activate
(venv) ~/Projects/httpbin-0.6.1$
```

2. Build the service in develop mode.

```
(venv) ~/Projects/httpbin-0.6.1$ python setup.py develop
running develop
running egg_info
writing httpbin.egg-info/PKG-INFO
####                    ####
#### removed for brevity ####
####                    ####
/Users/rahulsharma/Projects/httpbin-0.6.1/venv/bin
Using /Users/rahulsharma/Projects/httpbin-0.6.1/venv/lib/
python3.8/site-packages
Finished processing dependencies for httpbin==0.6.1
(venv) ~/Projects/httpbin-0.6.1$
```

3. Deploy the application in Gunicorn.

```
(venv) ~/Projects/httpbin-0.6.1$ gunicorn -b 0.0.0.0 httpbin:app
[2020-06-12 14:35:04 +0530] [67528] [INFO] Starting gunicorn 20.0.4
[2020-06-12 14:35:04 +0530] [67528] [INFO] Listening at:
   http://0.0.0.0:8000 (67528)
[2020-06-12 14:35:04 +0530] [67528] [INFO] Using worker: sync
[2020-06-12 14:35:04 +0530] [67530] [INFO] Booting worker with
pid: 67530
```

The httpbin service is now running on our system. You can access it at `http://localhost:8000` (see Figure 5-3). You can also test a few of the available endpoints.

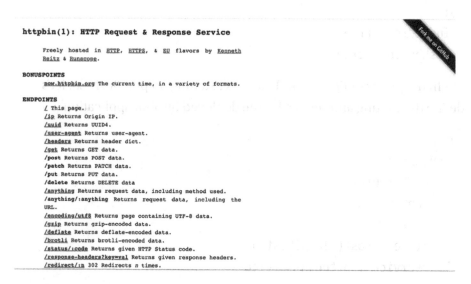

Figure 5-3. *httpbin service*

Traefik Configuration

In the previous section, we added an HTTP service. Let's now configure Traefik to send user requests to it. We will create the following `treafik.yml` with an entrypoint for web applications.

```
entryPoints :
  web :
    address : ":80"

providers :

    directory : /Users/rahulsharma/Projects/traefik-book/ch05/
                services
```

```
    watch : true
    filename : config
    debugLogGeneratedTemplate : true
api :
  insecure : true
  dashboard : true
```

In the prior configuration, Traefik is listening on port 80. Next, let's define the routing and service for the deployed httpbin application.

```
http :
 routers :
   guest-router :
     entryPoints :
     - web
     rule : Host(`localhost`)
     service : httpbin-service

 services :
   httpbin-service :
     loadBalancer :
       servers :
       - url  : http://192.168.1.4:8000/
```

This configuration sends requests to httpbin running on the 192.168.1.4 instance. This configuration needs to be copied to the services folder as config.yml. After this, you can look up http:// localhost. The browser should load the application. The deployed configuration can be seen on the Traefik dashboard (see Figure 5-4).

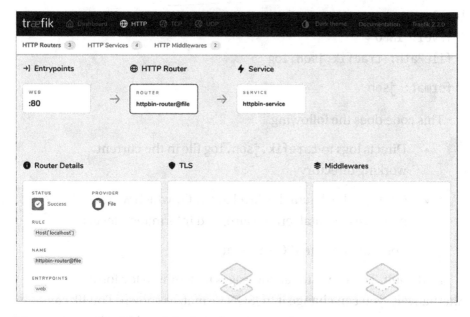

Figure 5-4. Dashboard for httpbin entrypoint

Traefik Logs

Traefik reports information about encountered issues. By default, Traefik reports these to standard output. These reported issues are corresponding to events in the Traefik application. The information is reported at different severity levels. You can configure Traefik logs by adding log configuration. The configuration can set up logging to a particular file. It can also specify the minimal severity level of messages.

```
entryPoints :
  web :
    address : ":80"

providers :
  # removed for Brevity
```

```
log:
  level: INFO
  filePath: traefik.json.log

format: json
```

This code does the following.

- Directs logs to `tarefik.json.log` file in the current working directory

- Changes the default log level to INFO, which writes messages for fatal, error, warn, and information levels

- Logs messages in JSON format

By default, Traefik writes all messages in common log format. Alternatively, you can change it to JSON format, as shown. Traefik can report log messages at the debug, info, warn, error, and fatal levels. Configuring a lower level enables reporting for all severity levels above the configured level.

The defined code is part of static configuration used to start Traefik. Traefik does not autoload these changes. Restart the server after making the changes. You can tail the log file as shown next.

```
ch05 $ tail -f traefik.json.log
{"level":"info","msg":"Traefik version 2.2.0 built on
2020-03-25T17:17:27Z","time":"2020-06-13T20:27:08+05:30"}
{"level":"info","msg":"\nStats collection is disabled.\nHelp
us improve Traefik by turning this feature on :)\nMore details
on: https://docs.traefik.io/contributing/data-collection/\
n","time":"2020-06-13T20:27:08+05:30"}
{"level":"error","msg":"unsupported access log format:
\"foobar\", defaulting to common format instead.","time":"2020-
06-13T20:27:08+05:30"}
```

{"level":"error","msg":"Failed to create new HTTP code ranges: strconv.Atoi: parsing \"foobar\": invalid syntax","time":"2020-06-13T20:27:08+05:30"}
{"level":"info","msg":"Starting provider aggregator. ProviderAggregator {}","time":"2020-06-13T20:27:08+05:30"}
{"level":"info","msg":"Starting provider *file.Provider {\"directory\":\"/Users/rahulsharma/Projects/traefik-book/ch05/code\",\"watch\":true,\"filename\":\"config\",\"debugLogGenerat edTemplate\":true}","time":"2020-06-13T20:27:08+05:30"}
{"level":"info","msg":"Starting provider *traefik.Provider {}","time":"2020-06-13T20:27:08+05:30"}

Access Logs

Traefik can report information about client requests. The information is written to access log after the request is processed. But the access log is not created by default. The access log configuration sets up logging to a particular file. But default access log is written in common log format. It can be configured to report in JSON format.

```
# Removed for Brevity

log:
  level: INFO
  filePath: traefik.json.log
  format: json

accessLog:
  filePath: access.json.log
  format: json
```

This code does the following.

- Directs access logs to access.json.log file in the current working directory

- Logs messages in JSON format

After adding the preceding configuration, restart the Traefik server. The following access logs are generated when we access http://localhost/.

```
logs $ tail -f access.json.log
{"ClientAddr":"[::1]:63226","ClientHost":"::1","ClientPort":"6
3226","ClientUsername":"-","DownstreamContentSize":12026,"Down
streamStatus":200,"Duration":28245000,"OriginContentSize":12026
,"OriginDuration":28187000,"OriginStatus":200,"Overhead":58000,
"RequestAddr":"localhost","RequestContentSize":0,"RequestCount"
:1,"RequestHost":"localhost","RequestMethod":"GET","RequestPat
h":"/","RequestPort":"-","RequestProtocol":"HTTP/1.1","Request
Scheme":"http","RetryAttempts":0,"RouterName":"httpbin-router@
file","ServiceAddr":"192.168.1.4:8000","ServiceName":"httpbin-
service@file","ServiceURL":{"Scheme":"http","Opaque":"","User":
null,"Host":"192.168.1.4:8000","Path":"/","RawPath":"","ForceQu
ery":false,"RawQuery":"","Fragment":""}
#### TRUNCATED }
```

The access logs contain diverse information. It can be helpful to determine outages and slow responses times by using the following reported attributes.

- Duration: The total time spent processing a request

- OriginDuration: The time spent between establishing a connection and receiving the last byte of the response body from the upstream server

- Overhead: The time difference between the response received from the upstream server and the response sent back to the client

- OriginStatus: The response code sent by the upstream server

```
"Duration":28245000,
"OriginContentSize":12026,
"OriginDuration":28187000,
"OriginStatus":200,
"Overhead":58000,
```

Since the access log is written after request processing, it adds overhead. But logging overheads can be optimized by configuring the buffer for the log messages. The buffer enables asynchronous write, instead of post-request write, of the log messages. The buffer specifies the number of log lines Traefik keeps in memory before writing them to the selected output. To enable the buffer, configure the buffersize attribute.

Note   The access log is a global configuration for only HTTP services. This is not an entrypoint or route-specific configuration. Once enabled, Traefik generates logs for all entrypoints/user requests.

Log Filters

Traefik access logs describe every request handled by the server. The information is detailed. The access log can grow very quickly if the server is handling many user requests. The large volume of information soon become unmanaged. Alternatively, you can log selective requests based on preconfigured criteria. This makes sure we are only looking at the relevant user requests. It excludes trivial log entries from the access log. The selective logging is enabled by using the filters attribute. The filter attribute provides the following three options.

- statusCodes: Logs only the specified list of response codes.

- retryAttempts: Logs when there are retry attempts

- minDuration: Logs when the request takes more than the specified time

```
# Removed for Brevity

accessLog:
  filePath: logs/access.json.log
  format: json
  bufferingSize: 50
  filters:
    statusCodes:
      - 200
      - 300-302
    retryAttempts: true
    minDuration: 5s
```

This code writes to access log when any of the following conditions is true .

- The response code is 200/300/301/302

- The request is retried using circuit breaks

- The request takes more than 5 seconds

Accessing http://localhost/ should generate a log message as the status code is 200. Now access http://localhost/status/418. There should not be any log statement.

```
logs $ tail -f access.json.log
{"ClientAddr":"[::1]:64020","ClientHost":"::1","ClientPort":"64
020","ClientUsername":"-","DownstreamContentSize":12026,"Downst
reamStatus":200,"Duration":27516000,"OriginContentSize":12026,"
```

```
OriginDuration":27467000,"OriginStatus":200,"Overhead":49000,
"RequestAddr":"localhost","RequestContentSize":0,"RequestCount":1,
"RequestHost":"localhost","RequestMethod":"GET","RequestPath":"/",
"RequestPort":"-","RequestProtocol":"HTTP/1.1","RequestScheme":
"http","RetryAttempts":0,"RouterName":"httpbin-router@file",
"ServiceAddr":"192.168.1.4:8000","ServiceName":"httpbin-
 service@file"...... TRUNCATED }
```

Log Fields

Previously, we discussed how you can log on response criteria. But Traefik can also be configured to report selective information in the log statements. You may be required to hide user identities, remove sensitive information, or optimize the log. Traefik log information consists of the following two types.

- Request headers: The headers passed by the user in the request

- Fields: Additional information added by Traefik

Both information types have attributes that can be controlled by the following options.

- keep reports as-is information in a log.

- drop removes the information from a log.

- redact replaces and masks information in a log.

```
accessLog:
  filePath: logs/access.json.log
  format: json
  bufferingSize: 50
  fields:
    defaultMode: keep
```

```
names:
  ClientUsername: drop
headers:
  defaultMode: keep
  names:
      User-Agent: redact
      Authorization: drop
      Content-Type: keep
```

In this code, we configured the following.

- The keep value for defaultmode enables the reporting
  of fields and headers.

- The keep value for defaultmode enables reporting
  headers.

- The drop value for ClientUsername removes it from a log.

- The drop value for Content-Type and Authorization
  removes these headers from a log.

- The redact value for User-Agent reports the value as
  redacted.

After adding the preceding configuration, restart the Traefik server.
The following access logs are generated when you access http://localhost/.

```
logs $ tail -f access.json.log
{"ClientAddr":"[::1]:49537","ClientHost":"::1","ClientPort":"49537",

<!-- REMOVED for Brevity -->

,"origin_X-Processed-Time":"0","request_Accept":"text/
html,application/xhtml+xml,application/xml;q=0.9,image/
webp,image/apng,*/*;q=0.8,application/signed-
exchange;v=b3;q=0.9","request_Accept-Encoding":"gzip, deflate,
```

br","request_Accept-Language":"en-US,en;q=0.9","request_
Cache-Control":"max-age=0","request_Connection":"keep-
alive","request_Sec-Fetch-Dest":"document","request_Sec-Fetch-
Mode":"navigate","request_Sec-Fetch-Site":"none","request_
Sec-Fetch-User":"?1","request_Upgrade-Insecure-
Requests":"1","request_User-Agent":"REDACTED","request_X-
Forwarded-Host":"localhost","request_X-
Forwarded-Port":"80","request_X-Forwarded-
Proto":"http","request_X-Forwarded-Server":"XE-GGN-IT-02498.
local","request_X-Real-Ip":"::1","time":"2020-06-
14T16:35:18+05:30"}

Note   Traefik reports about 25 additional fields. The list of fields is available in Traefik documentation.

Log Rotation

Production deployed applications prefer the policy of log rotation. This helps in optimal disk usage as historical logs are purged. But Traefik logs are not rotated by default. Thus we need to use system programs to perform log management. Logs management involves archiving and purging activities. Depending on the operating system, there are various programs to do this. On FreeBSD systems, you can use newsyslog, while on Linux, you can use logrotate. All of them rely on sending USR1 signals to rotate logs. In the following discussion, we work with newsyslog. The outlined steps remain the same for any other program.

The newsyslog utility included in FreeBSD rotates, and archives log files, if necessary. The program needs input in for a configuration file. The file identifies which all log files need to be handled. It provides a diverse set of attributes that can describe the file permissions, copy behavior, archive count, and so forth. The program is configured to run at periodic intervals by using a scheduling program like `crontab`. Let's create the following configuration in a file named syslog.conf.

```
/Users/rahulsharma/Projects/traefik-book/ch05/logs/access.json.
log    rahulsharma:staff    640 5    500    *    Z
```

In this configuration, we configured log rotation for `acces.json.log`.

- Set the file owner and group to `rahulsharma:staff`. This applies to the zipped file and the new log file.

- Set the file permission to 640.

- There are only five rotations for the file.

- The rotation happens when the size grows above 500,000.

- The Z flag configures zipped files.

You can run `newsyslog` with the described configuration using the following command.

```
code $ sudo newsyslog -vf  syslog.conf
/Users/rahulsharma/Projects/traefik-book/ch05/logs/access.json.
log <5Z>: size (Kb): 532 [500] --> trimming log....
Signal all daemon process(es)...
Notified daemon pid 91 = /var/run/syslog.pid
Pause 10 seconds to allow daemon(s) to close log file(s)
Compress all rotated log file(s)...
```

Note   The preceding process does not apply to Windows because there is no log rotate program due to a lack of USR signals.

Blacklisting

Traefik provides support for backlisting by using middleware. We discussed middleware in Chapter 2. They are configured as part of routers. Middleware is executed after the rule matching but before forwarding the request to the service. Traefik supports IP backlisting by configuring ipWhiteList middleware. It can be configured by using the following options.

- sourceRange: Describes the set of allowed IPs in CIDR format

- ipstrategy: Describes how to identify client IP from the X-forward-for header

```
http :
  routers :
    httpbin-router :
      entryPoints :
      - web
      rule : HostRegexp(`{name:.*}`)
      middlewares :
      - allowed-sources
      service : httpbin-service

  middlewares:
    allowed-sources:
      ipWhiteList:
        sourceRange:
          - "127.0.0.1/32"

  services :
  # Removed for Brevity
```

In the preceding code, we did the following.

- We modified to router rule to allow all hostnames using a regular expression. This is done using the HostRegexp function instead of the Host operator.

- We added the Middlewares section with the name of the configured ipWhiteList middleware.

- We configured the Middlewares section with the configuration for ipWhiteList.

- We added the list of allowed IPs using the sourceRange option.

Now let's run the configuration. Access the http://localhost/ page to access the httpbin service.

```
$ curl -v http://localhost/
*   Trying ::1...
* TCP_NODELAY set
* Connected to localhost (::1) port 80 (#0)
> GET / HTTP/1.1
> Host: localhost
> User-Agent: curl/7.64.1
> Accept: */*
>
< HTTP/1.1 403 Forbidden
< Date: Sat, 20 Jun 2020 17:41:11 GMT
< Content-Length: 9
< Content-Type: text/plain; charset=utf-8
<
* Connection #0 to host localhost left intact
Forbidden* Closing connection 0
```

We get back a forbidden response. This is so because our localhost domain is resolved to the IP6 loopback address (::1). The loopback address is not in the whitelist. Alternatively, you can access using the IP4 loopback address (127.0.0.1). This should load the page as expected. The forbidden access is reported in access logs. Make sure that you remove status code-based log filters from the static configuration.

```
{"ClientAddr":"[::1]:64616","ClientHost":"::1","ClientPort
":"64616","ClientUsername":"-","DownstreamContentSize":9,"
DownstreamStatus":403,"Duration":128000,"OriginContentSiz
e":9,"OriginDuration":79000,"OriginStatus":403,"Overhead"
:49000,"RequestAddr":"localhost","RequestContentSize":0,"
RequestCount":63,"RequestHost":"localhost","RequestMethod
":"GET","RequestPath":"/","RequestPort":"-","RequestProto
col":"HTTP/1.1","RequestScheme":"http","RetryAttempts":0,
"RouterName":"httpbin-router@file","StartLocal":"2020-06-
20T23:11:01.21434+05:30","StartUTC":"2020-06-20T17:41:01.21434
Z","entryPointName":"web","level":"info","msg":"","time":"2020-
06-20T23:11:01+05:30"}
```

Request Tracing

You learned that observability is a diverse practice. Request tracing or distributed tracing is an important pillar to profile application behaviors. It is commonly applied to distributed systems to project how the request processing has happened across different systems. It can point out applications that have caused performance issues or have failed request processing.

In a nutshell, distributed tracing maps the flow of a request as it is processed through a system. The processing flow is created on a building block known as a *request span*. A request span represents time spent in processing by a service. All services which process the request generate their individual spans. These spans are then combined into a single distributed trace for the entire request.

As an API gateway, Traefik receives incoming requests for different applications. It is the single point of entry for all external requests. Traefik must support the generation of request spans. The generated request spans are propagated as request headers to the application. In turn, the application must propagate these headers further. Traefik generates the following B3 trace headers.

- x-b3-traceid

- x-b3-spanid

- x-b3-parentspanid

- x-b3-sampled

These spans are sent to a tracing backend service. The service is responsible for storing and processing this information. Traefik supports several OpenTracing backends like Zipkin, Datadog, and Jagger. In this section, we work with Zipkin. Similar configurations are required for other backends.

Install Zipkin

Zipkin is an open source trace collection engine built in Java. It not only supports trace collection, but it also provides a dashboard to visualize traces. There are other features that allow you to analyze request flows. Since Zipkin is open sourced, it provides access to code that can be compiled for a target platform. Alternatively, we directly run a released binary. Zipkin's latest release can be downloaded using the following command.

```
code $curl -sSL https://zipkin.io/quickstart.sh | bash -s
Thank you for trying Zipkin!
This installer is provided as a quick-start helper, so you can
try Zipkin out
without a lengthy installation process.

Fetching version number of latest io.zipkin:zipkin-server release...
Latest release of io.zipkin:zipkin-server seems to be 2.21.4

Downloading io.zipkin:zipkin-server:2.21.4:exec to zipkin.jar...
```

Once zipkin.jar is downloaded, run it using the following command.

```
code $ java -jar zipkin.jar
2020-06-20 21:57:31.012  INFO 47685 --- [           main] z.s
.ZipkinServer                   : Starting ZipkinServer
on XE-GGN-IT-02498.local with PID 47685 (/Users/rahulsharma/
Projects/trafik/code/zipkin.jar started by rahulsharma in /
Users/rahulsharma/Projects/trafik/code)
2020-06-20 21:57:31.016  INFO 47685 --- [           main] z.s.
ZipkinServer                    : The following profiles
are active: shared
2020-06-20 21:57:32.040  INFO 47685 --- [           main] c.
l.a.c.u.SystemInfo              : hostname: xe-ggn-
it-02498.local (from 'hostname' command)
2020-06-20 21:57:32.537  INFO 47685 --- [oss-http-*:9411] c.
l.a.s.Server                    : Serving HTTP at
/0:0:0:0:0:0:0:0:9411 - http://127.0.0.1:9411/
2020-06-20 21:57:32.538  INFO 47685 --- [           main] c.l.a.s.
ArmeriaAutoConfiguration        : Armeria server started at ports:
{/0:0:0:0:0:0:0:0:9411=ServerPort(/0:0:0:0:0:0:0:0:9411, [http])}
```

The server is up and running on 9411 port. You can access its
dashboard at http://localhost:9411/.

Figure 5-5. *Zipkin dashboard*

Integrate Zipkin

Traefik integration with Zipkin is simple. We only need to provide
the Zipkin API location. The parameters are part of Traefik's static
configuration. Traefik also provides the following attributes to customize
the tracing behavior.

- sameSpan: Configures one span for RPC invocations

- id128Bit: Generates 128-bit trace IDs

- samplerate: Percentage of requests traced

```
# Removed for Brevity

tracing:
  zipkin:
    httpEndpoint: http://localhost:9411/api/v2/spans
    id128Bit : true
    sameSpan: true
```

In this configuration, we provided the location for the Zipkin API. We also configured 128-bit traces with the same span for RPC client and server. Now restart the server.

```
ch05 $ traefik  --configfile traefik.yml
INFO[0000] Configuration loaded from file: /Users/rahulsharma/
Projects/traefik-book/ch05/traefik.yml
```

You can validate the configuration in the Traefik dashboard (see Figure 5-6). It should report which tracing backend is configured in the application.

Note   Tracing is enabled at a global level. Once enabled, it generates traces for all requests, including the dashboard API.

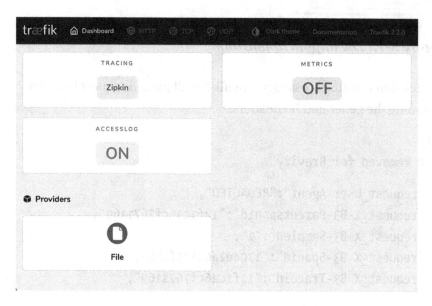

Figure 5-6. *Tracing dashboard status*

Now, let's make a couple of requests. The httpbin application (see Figure 5-7) provides several request types. Try loading the IP, status code, and redirect requests. Traefik generates the request traces and sends it to the deployed Zipkin.

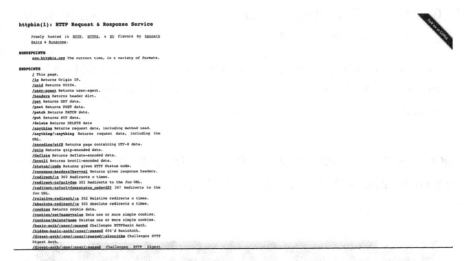

Figure 5-7. *The httpbin application*

You can tail the access logs. Traefik log all passed request headers, including the generated B3 headers.

```
{
# Removed for Brevity

"request_User-Agent":"REDACTED",
"request_X-B3-Parentspanid":"12f1ca6cf7671169",
"request_X-B3-Sampled":"1",
"request_X-B3-Spanid":"1704e2a62f95fa8b",
"request_X-B3-Traceid":"12f1ca6cf7671169",
}
```

Traefik integration consists of the following steps.

- Generate TraceId and Span for a request based on the configured sampling rate

- Forward the trace headers to the service application

- Update the spans based on the response code

- Send the generated trace spans to the tracing backend

Now, you can load the Zipkin dashboard. The dashboard provides a UI to visualize request traces. You can search for requests during the last 15 mins. The resulting page should look as per the following. The tracer/ Zipkin dashboard(see Figure 5-8) marks all traces with 2XX or 3XX return in blue. But a return code of 4XX /5XX is shown in red.

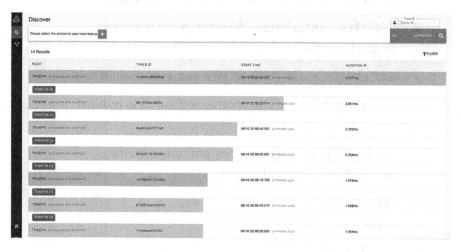

Figure 5-8. *Request traces*

Traefik Metrics

Traefik can generate application-level metrics. These metrics must be captured in a backed service for monitoring and alert notifications. Traefik supports the most widely used metrics solutions like StatsD, Datadog, Prometheus, and so forth. In the current section, we work with Prometheus as a metrics-backed store. Prometheus is an open-source solution built using Golang. Prometheus can scrape metrics from endpoints exposed in Traefik. It also provides a dashboard to visualize metrics. Prometheus details are beyond the scope of the book.

Let's first enable Traefik metrics by adding a relevant configuration. The configuration needs to be added to the static-configuration file. Traefik provides the following options.

- buckets: Defines buckets for response latencies

- addEntryPointLabels: Adds entrypoint names to request metrics

- addServiceLabels: Adds service names to request metrics

- entryPoint: Names entrypoint configured to publish metrics

- manualrouting: Enables a custom router for the prometheus@internal service

```
entryPoints :
  web :
    address : ":80"

# Removed for Brevity

metrics:
  prometheus:
    addEntryPointsLabels: true
    addServicesLabels : true
```

This configuration enables metrics on the default endpoint. The metrics are generated at `http://locahost:8080/metrics`. Restart the server and verify the configuration on the Traefik dashboard.

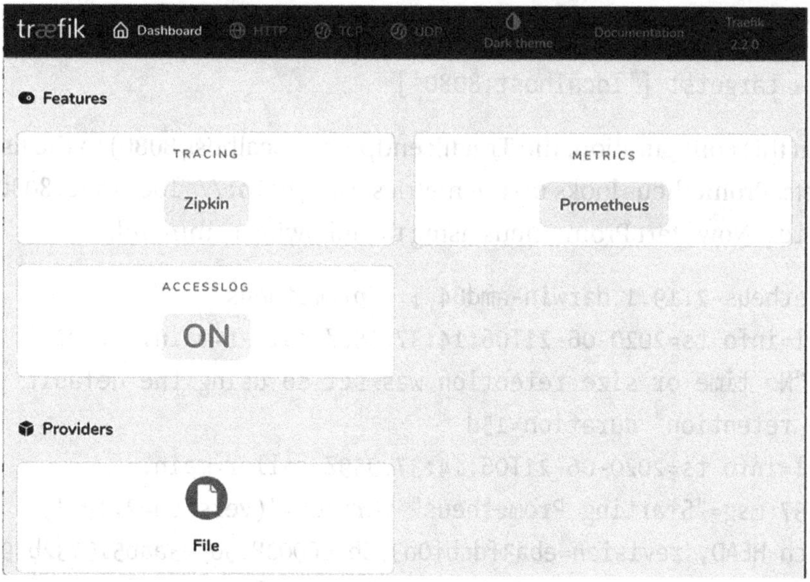

Figure 5-9. Enable metrics

Configure Prometheus

Now we need to capture the generated metrics in Prometheus. Let's start by downloading the latest version using the Release page (`https://prometheus.io/download/`). You can unzip the release. But before starting the Prometheus server, we need to configure the endpoint, which needs to be scrapped. This can be done by updating the bundled `prometheus.yml`

```
# my global config
global:
  scrape_interval:     15s # Set the scrape interval to every
  15 seconds. Default is every 1 minute.
```

```
evaluation_interval: 15s # Evaluate rules every 15 seconds.
The default is every 1 minute.
# scrape_timeout is set to the global default (10s).
```

REMOVED for BREVITY

```
  static_configs:
  - targets: ['localhost:8080']
```

In this configuration, the Traefik endpoint (localhost:8080) to the list of targets. Prometheus looks up the metrics using http:// localhot:8080/ metrics. Now start Prometheus using the following command.

```
prometheus-2.19.1.darwin-amd64 $ ./prometheus
level=info ts=2020-06-21T06:14:37.958Z caller=main.go:302
msg="No time or size retention was set so using the default
time retention" duration=15d
level=info ts=2020-06-21T06:14:37.959Z caller=main.
go:337 msg="Starting Prometheus" version="(version=2.19.1,
branch=HEAD, revision=eba3fdcbf0d378b66600281903e3aab515732b39)"
level=info ts=2020-06-21T06:14:37.959Z caller=main.go:338
build_context="(go=go1.14.4, user=root@62700b3d0ef9,
date=20200618-16:45:01)"
level=info ts=2020-06-21T06:14:37.959Z caller=main.go:339
host_details=(darwin)
level=info ts=2020-06-21T06:14:37.959Z caller=main.go:340
fd_limits="(soft=2560, hard=unlimited)"
level=info ts=2020-06-21T06:14:37.959Z caller=main.go:341
vm_limits="(soft=unlimited, hard=unlimited)"
level=info ts=2020-06-21T06:14:37.960Z caller=main.go:678
msg="Starting TSDB ..."
level=info ts=2020-06-21T06:14:37.960Z caller=web.
go:524 component=web msg="Start listening for connections"
address=0.0.0.0:9090
```

We can Load Prometheus dashboard using `http://localhost:9090/`. The metric dropdown have different options with `traefik_` prefix. We load the `traefik_entrypoint_requests_total` metric. It described the total number of requests handler by Traefik. Additionally, you can also send several requests to Traefik using the following bash script.

```
$ for ((i=1;i<=10000;i++)); do   curl -v --header "Connection:
keep-alive" "localhost"; done
```

This script sends about 10,000 requests to Traefik server. Lastly, you can check the Prometheus dashboard (see Figure 5-10), which captures the growth in traffic.

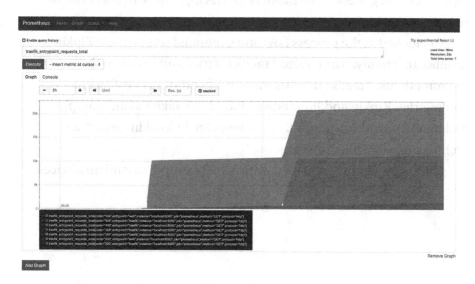

Figure 5-10. *Request traffic metric*

Summary

This chapter discussed observability. We talked about its three pillars of error logs, request traces, and application metrics. First, we configured error logs. These logs capture information about any errors occurring in Traefik. As a next step, we configured access logs. The access logs capture incoming requests handled by Traefik. As the incoming requests increase, the access logs can bloat quickly.

We discussed ways to manage it by using filters, rotation, and header masking. We also configured IPwhitelist middleware and captured the forbidden logs generated by it. After this, we enabled request tracing using Zipkin. Traefik generates B3 headers for tracing. These headers can be seen in access logs.

You looked at the process flow and generated traces in the Zipkin dashboard. Finally, we enabled Traefik metrics and captured them in Prometheus. Traefik supports many backend stores for Tracing and metrics. Zipkin and Prometheus have been taken as an example to demonstrate its integration. These tools are helpful in distributed architectures like microservices.

In the next chapter, you work with Traefik support for microservices.

CHAPTER 6

Traefik for Microservices

In Chapter 1, we discussed microservice architecture. Businesses are increasingly moving away from the monolith architecture to take advantage of the microservice architecture. But a microservices system is a distributed system. To use it efficiently, we need to adopt additional infrastructure components. These additional components prescribe a new set of guidelines that must be followed with each microservice.

Microservice architecture advocates granule services for evolving business needs. Depending on changing business needs, development teams can create or combine services. Moreover, in the production environment, each of the services is deployed and scaled independently. Cloud-based autoscaling often replicates instances based on service load. Thus, the architecture is in constant evolution, and there is no end-state list of microservices.

A dynamic ecosystem requires a catalog of the latest running microservices. This is also known as the *service registry*. In a nutshell, the registry is a database of services with details of their instances and the corresponding locations. To work efficiently, services must be registered on startup and removed on shutdown. There are many ways to achieve this, but the process of service self-registration is the recommended mechanism.

© Rahul Sharma, Akshay Mathur 2021
R. Sharma and A. Mathur, *Traefik API Gateway for Microservices*,
https://doi.org/10.1007/978-1-4842-6376-1_6

Once the services are registered with the registry, a client needs a lookup for the same service. This client-side process is known as service discovery (see Figure 6-1). The client first queries the service registry to find the available instances of a service. After getting the list of active service instances, the client can send a request to the required service.

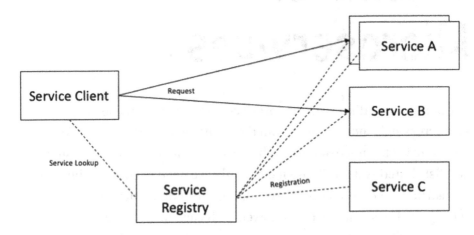

Figure 6-1. *Service registration and service discovery*

The service registry is often a key-value store of information. Many times, you must register additional information about the service. This information can be related to the client's type in a multitenant system, or the view provided, like web or mobile, or any other information. Every service is responsible for adding this data to the store. In this chapter, we use the service self-registration mechanism to integrate Traefik with the microservices.

Microservice architecture recommends service collaboration. This means that one service can invoke other services to get the required data for a user request. But the mechanism has its own set of issues. When one service synchronously invokes another service, there is always the possibility that the other service is unavailable or is exhibiting such high latency that it is essentially unusable.

Precious resources such as threads might be consumed in the caller while waiting for the other service to respond. This might lead to resource exhaustion, which would make the calling service unable to handle other requests.

The failure of one service can potentially cascade to other services throughout the application. The problem can be fixed by adapting circuit breakers (see Figure 6-2) in the application design. When the number of consecutive failures crosses a threshold, the circuit breaker trips, and for the duration of a timeout period, all attempts to invoke the remote service fail immediately.

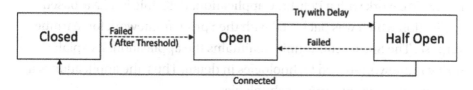

Figure 6-2. *Circuit breaker pattern*

After the timeout expires, the circuit breaker allows a limited number of test requests to pass through. If those requests succeed, the circuit breaker resumes normal operation. Otherwise, if there is a failure, the timeout period begins again. In this chapter, we integrate circuit breakers while invoking different microservices from Traefik.

API gateways are an essential part of any microservice-based architecture. Cross-cutting concerns such as authentication, load balancing, dependency resolution, data transformations, and dynamic request dispatching can be handled conveniently and generically. Microservices can then focus on their specific tasks without code duplication. This results in easier and faster development of each microservice.

Implement an API gateway that is the single entry point for all clients. The API gateway handles requests in one of two ways. Some requests are proxied/routed to the appropriate service. It handles other requests by fanning out to multiple services. In previous chapters, we configured Traefik for the requirements for single services. In this chapter, we configure Traefik as a microservices gateway.

Pet-Clinic Application

In this chapter, we need a microservices-based application. The application must have at least two or more microservices integrated with Traefik. We work with a PetClinic application. PetClinic is a Java-based application which was packaged with the Spring framework for learning purpose. The Spring community maintains the application. It explains Spring framework-based technologies in detail. Thus, the application is a good test-bed for enterprise technologies.

The PetClinic application is designed for the needs of a veterinary clinic. The application enables its users to view and manage veterinarians, customers, and their pets. The application supports the following use cases.

- View a list of veterinarians and their specialties

- View information about a pet owner

- Update the information about a pet owner

- Add a new pet owner to the system

- View information about a pet

- Update the information about a pet

- Add a new pet to the system

- View information about a pet's visitation history

- Add information about a visit to the pet's visitation history

The solution needs to be built using microservice architecture. Let's download the PetClinic application from `https://github.com/rahul0208/spring-petclinic-microservices`.

Spring PetClinic microservices are built around small independent services (a few hundred lines of code), running in their own JVM and communicating over HTTP via a REST API. These microservices are all written in Java. Each of the three customer, vet, and visit business microservices is an application in the Spring Boot sense. To work in a distributed environment, these microservices rely on a set of tools offered by Spring Cloud: centralized configuration management, automated discovery of other microservices, and load balancing (see Figure 6-3). The application UI is developed in Angular and deployed in Nginx. Traefik will perform request-routing. We build and deploy an application in this chapter. Some important aspects are covered, but complete application technical details are beyond the scope of the book.

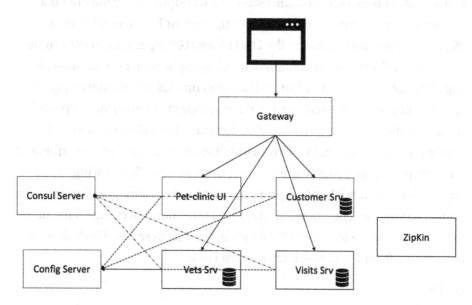

Figure 6-3. *PetClinic services*

Application Configuration

The PetClinic application configuration is at `https://github.com/ rahul0208/spring-petclinic-microservices-config`. The configuration is served using the spring-cloud-config server. The config server makes the configuration available at the following REST URLs.

- /{application}/{profile}[/{label}]

- /{application}-{profile}.yml

- /{label}/{application}-{profile}.yml

- /{application}-{profile}.properties

- /{label}/{application}-{profile}.properties

The config-server also removes the requirement of repackaging the application in the event of configuration changes. Since all the latest configuration is available on the listed REST endpoints, we only need a service restart. Services can also be configured for hot-reload by using `@RefreshScope` annotation or the `EnvironmentChangeEvent` event listener.

Spring follows the convention of loading application configuration from `application.properties`. But as discussed previously, when the spring-cloud-config server is used, `application.properties` is no longer part of the application. Instead, a spring-cloud-context is configured to load the configuration properties from the external sources. It can also be configured for decrypting properties in the external configuration files. Spring Cloud application initiates a bootstrap context that loads its configuration from the bootstrap.yml file. The bootstrap.yml file is minimalist. It contains the name of the microservice and the URL of the configuration server. The following is an example from the vets-service microservice.

```
spring:
  cloud:
    config:
```

```
    uri: http://localhost:8888
  application:
    name: vets-service
```

We specified the spring-config-server location at localhost:8888 in the configuration. The vets-service microservice requires the server to be up on the said location. It queries the server to determine the configuration values and then complete the server startup. It is important to note that the config server's location can be injected using environment variables like SPRING_CLOUD_CONFIG. But it can't be discovered using the service registry.

Consul Service Registry

Previously we discussed the evolving nature of microservice architecture. When services are deployed in the cloud, you can hardly anticipate the number of instances of the same microservices (depending on the load) or where they are deployed (and on which IP and port they are accessible). Thus, there is a need for a service registry. In the PetClinic application, we used the Consul service registry. At startup, each microservices registers itself with the service registry. Post-registration, each service periodically provides a heartbeat to the registry. The book does not aim to cover details around the Consul service registry. Please refer to the documentation for more information.

Now let's download consul from `www.consul.io/`. Post-download, extract the zipped file and start the service.

```
$ ./consul agent -dev
==> Starting Consul agent...
           Version: 'v1.8.0'
           Node ID: '935fccd6-74ca-e62e-c53f-c838de3c3681'
         Node name: 'XE-GGN-IT-02498.local'
        Datacenter: 'dc1' (Segment: '<all>')
            Server: true (Bootstrap: false)
       Client Addr: [127.0.0.1] (HTTP: 8500, HTTPS: -1, gRPC:
       8502, DNS: 8600)
      Cluster Addr: 127.0.0.1 (LAN: 8301, WAN: 8302)
           Encrypt: Gossip: false, TLS-Outgoing: false, TLS-
           Incoming: false, Auto-Encrypt-TLS: false

==> Log data will now stream in as it occurs:
```

We can load the Consul UI at http://localhost:8500/ui/dc1/services. (see Figure 6-4)

Figure 6-4. *Consul services*

Deploy Pet-Clinic

Now we can run the PetClinic microservices in any order. The application consists of the following three microservices.

- Vets service

- Visits service

- Customer service

All the services are based on Spring Boot. They are packaged as executable JAR files. Executing the service-specific jar starts the service with an embedded servlet engine. Since the service fetches are configuration from the spring-config server, so let's make sure that we are the correct location of the config server in bootstrap.yml.

Next, make sure that the config-server points to the correct git location. In the example, `https://github.com/rahul0208/spring-petclinic-microservices-config` is the application configuration source. We recommended that you clone this configuration and update it per the environment.

The preceding URL is configured in bootstrap.yml for config-server.

```
server.port: 8888
spring:
  cloud:
    config:
      server:
        git:
          uri: https://github.com/spring-petclinic/spring-
              petclinic-microservices-config
        native:
          searchLocations: file:///${GIT_REPO}
```

The details of the configuration are beyond the scope of this book. We recommend that you update the URI with its own clone. Now, we need to build the services using the packages maven wrapper.

```
$ ./mvnw clean install
[INFO] Scanning for projects...
[INFO] ------------------------------------------------------------
[INFO] Reactor Build Order:
[INFO]
[INFO] spring-petclinic-microservic
es                                    [pom]
[INFO] spring-petclinic-customers-servi
ce                                    [jar]
[INFO] spring-petclinic-vets-service
                                      [jar]
[INFO] spring-petclinic-visits-service
                                      [jar]
[INFO] spring-petclinic-config-server
                                      [jar]
...
..... Truncated for Brevity
```

The command creates an executable for each service under the target folder.

```
$ find  . -type f  -name "*jar"
./spring-petclinic-config-server/target/spring-petclinic-
config-server-2.3.1.jar
./spring-petclinic-ui/target/spring-petclinic-ui-2.3.1.jar
./spring-petclinic-vets-service/target/spring-petclinic-vets-
service-2.3.1.jar
./.mvn/wrapper/maven-wrapper.jar
```

```
./spring-petclinic-customers-service/target/spring-petclinic-
customers-service-2.3.1.jar
./spring-petclinic-visits-service/target/spring-petclinic-
visits-service-2.3.1.jar
```

In the current setup, we deployed all services in the same box. Thus, localhost address is used in the configuration. You are free to deploy the service on any host, by making an appropriate update in their git config. As a first step, you need to start the config server with the following command.

```
target $ java -jar spring-petclinic-config-server-2.3.1.jar
2020-07-26 21:56:26.401  INFO 7442 --- [              main]
o.s.s.p.config.ConfigServerApplication   : No active profile
set, falling back to default profiles: default
2020-07-26 21:56:27.221  INFO 7442 --- [              main]
o.s.cloud.context.scope.GenericScope     : BeanFactory
id=15cd0375-3bcf-3529-9d02-67397a0dc277
2020-07-26 21:56:27.609  INFO 7442 --- [              main]
o.s.b.w.embedded.tomcat.TomcatWebServer  : Tomcat initialized
with port(s): 8888 (http)
2020-07-26 21:56:27.621  INFO 7442 --- [              main]
o.apache.catalina.core.StandardService   : Starting service
[Tomcat]
2020-07-26 21:56:27.621  INFO 7442 --- [              main] org.
apache.catalina.core.StandardEngine  : Starting Servlet engine:
[Apache Tomcat/9.0.36]
2020-07-26 21:56:27.690  INFO 7442 --- [              main]
```

The next step is to run each microservice. But first let's make sure that we have the correct address of the Consul service registry in application.yml.

```
spring:
  cloud:
    consul:
      host: localhost
      port: 8500
```

Let's now start the vets-service with the following command.

```
target $ java -jar spring-petclinic-vets-service-2.3.1.jar
2020-07-21 15:34:11.693  INFO [vets-service,,,] 26509 ---
[             main] c.c.c.ConfigServicePropertySourceLocator :
Fetching config from server at : http://localhost:8888
2020-07-21 15:34:15.525  INFO [vets-service,,,] 26509 --- [
main] c.c.c.ConfigServicePropertySourceLocator : Located
environment: name=vets-service, profiles=[default], label=null,
version=062fb94b71dc6b99e6518fe7088a0bff3a9431d1, state=null
2020-07-21 15:34:15.527  INFO [vets-service,,,] 26509 ---
[             main] b.c.PropertySourceBootstrapConfigurat
ion : Located property source: [BootstrapPropertySource
{name='bootstrapProperties-configClient'},
BootstrapPropertySource {name='bootstrapProperties-
https://github.com/spring-petclinic/spring-petclinic-
microservices-config/vets-service.yml (document #1)'},
BootstrapPropertySource {name='bootstrapProperties-
https://github.com/spring-petclinic/spring-petclinic-
microservices-config/vets-service.yml (document #0)'},
BootstrapPropertySource {name='bootstrapProperties-https://
github.com/spring-petclinic/spring-petclinic-microservices-
config/application.yml (document #0)'}]
- Start completed.
```

Similarly, we need to start the customer-service and visits services. Each service registers itself in the Consul service registry. You can validate the service details in the Consul dashboard (see Figure 6-5). Additionally, each of these services may report a failure for the Zipkin-based request tracing. Request tracing offers various benefits. In Chapter 5, we covered the integration of these tools with Traefik. We do not cover these integrations in this chapter.

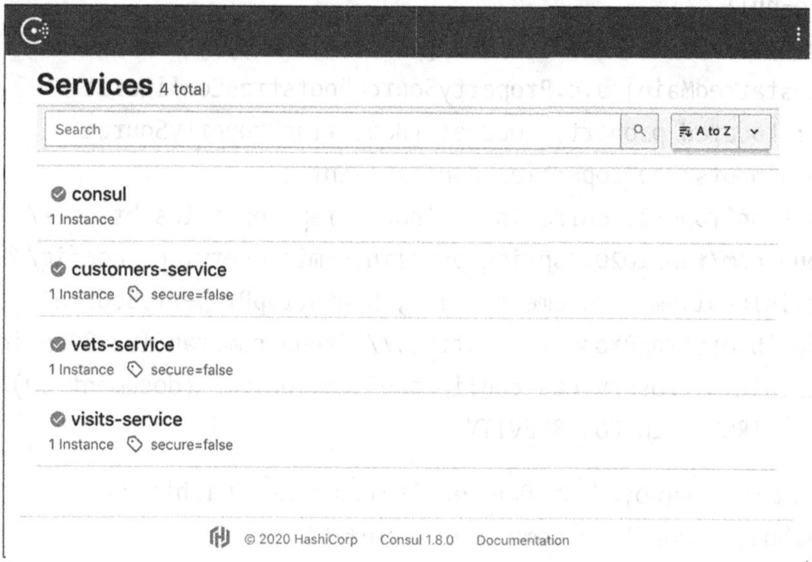

Figure 6-5. *Dashboard UI*

Pet-Clinic UI

The application UI is built using 1.7 version on AngularJS. These HTML pages are deployed as static resources of a Spring web Application. Alternatively, we can pack and deploy them in a server like Apache Tomcat or HTTPD. The UI is also packaged as an executable JAR. Let's now start the UI with the following command.

```
target $ java -jar spring-petclinic-ui-2.3.1.jar
2020-07-27 22:15:21.996  INFO [petclinic-ui,,,] 17732 ---
[  restartedMain] c.c.c.ConfigServicePropertySourceLocator :
Fetching config from server at : http://localhost:8888
2020-07-27 22:15:22.870  INFO [petclinic-ui,,,] 17732 ---
[  restartedMain] c.c.c.ConfigServicePropertySourceLocator :
Located environment: name=petclinic-ui, profiles=[default],
label=null, version=8adeb754f96df6e7308344e7bb2ceddcca09b93f,
state=null
2020-07-27 22:15:22.871  INFO [petclinic-ui,,,] 17732 ---
[  restartedMain] b.c.PropertySourceBootstrapConfigurat
ion : Located property source: [BootstrapPropertySource
{name='bootstrapProperties-configClient'},
BootstrapPropertySource {name='bootstrapProperties-https://
github.com/rahul0208/spring-petclinic-microservices-config/
petclinic-ui.yml (document #0)'}, BootstrapPropertySource
{name='bootstrapProperties-https://github.com/rahul0208/spring-
petclinic-microservices-config/application.yml (document #0)'}]
...... TRUNCATED FOR BREVITY
```

The UI is deployed on 9000 port. We can access it as http://
localhost:9000/#!/welcome. (see Figure 6-6)

Figure 6-6. *PetClinic UI*

The UI is also updating the Consul service registry. This way, the registry is a comprehensive catalog of the running services.

Configure Gateway

In the preceding setup, we deployed all microservices of the application. Now we need to configure Traefik to render the UI and route calls to each service. We can write this configuration in a file as done in previous chapters. It configures Traefik, but the approach does not work with the dynamic nature of the microservice architecture. We would need to keep updating the configuration as a new service gets added to the ecosystem. Also, it is difficult to keep updating the IP address of all instances of a service.

Alternatively, Traefik can be used with Consul key-value store as a configuration provider. All Traefik configuration is added hierarchically as key and values under a configured root node. The default root node is named "traefik". Table 6-1 highlights some of the Traefik keys.

Table 6-1. Keys for Traefik

Key	Value
traefik/http/routers/<route-name>/entryPoints/0	Specifies respective entrypoint name
traefik/http/routers/<route-name>/middlewares/0	Specifies the middleware name
traefik/http/routers/<route-name>/rule	Specifies the matching rule
traefik/http/routers/<route-name>/service	Specifies the respective service name
traefik/http/service/<service-name>/loadbalancers/0/url	Specifies the instance URL location
raefik/http/middlewares/<middleware-name>/stripPrefix/prefixes/0	Specifies the middleware configuration

Traefik documentation provides the updated list of keys to configure it. As a first step, let's add the configuration to Consul. You can create it using Consul GUI. Alternatively, you can import keys from a JSON file. The values for each key are encoded in Base64 format.

```
$ consul kv import "$(cat config.json)"
Imported: traefik/http/middlewares/petclinic-customers-
stripprefix/stripPrefix/prefixes/0
Imported: traefik/http/middlewares/petclinic-visits-
stripprefix/stripPrefix/prefixes/0
Imported: traefik/http/routers/petclinic-customers-route/
entryPoints/0
```

```
Imported: traefik/http/routers/petclinic-customers-route/
middlewares/0
Imported: traefik/http/routers/petclinic-customers-route/rule
Imported: traefik/http/routers/petclinic-customers-route/service
Imported: traefik/http/routers/petclinic-route/entryPoints/0
Imported: traefik/http/routers/petclinic-route/rule
Imported: traefik/http/routers/petclinic-route/service
Imported: traefik/http/routers/petclinic-vets-route/entryPoints/0
Imported: traefik/http/routers/petclinic-vets-route/rule
Imported: traefik/http/routers/petclinic-vets-route/service
Imported: traefik/http/routers/petclinic-visits-route/entryPoints/0
Imported: traefik/http/routers/petclinic-visits-route/middlewares/0
Imported: traefik/http/routers/petclinic-visits-route/rule
Imported: traefik/http/routers/petclinic-visits-route/service
```

Once the configuration is imported, we should see all key-values in the Consul store. Now we need to update the Traefik static configuration to use Consul provider.

```
entryPoints :
  web :
    address : ":80"

providers:
  consul:
    endpoints:
      - "127.0.0.1:8500"
    rootKey : "traefik"

api :
  insecure : true
  dashboard : true
```

175

We specified the Consul provider instead of FileProvider in the configuration. We also specified the location and the root key. There are additional options to configure authentication and TLS information. Let's start the Traefik server and look up the dashboard.

Figure 6-7. *Traefik configuration from Consul*

The dashboard shows the configuration from Consul key-value store. Traefik has created four new routes, one for each deployed service. If the services are not running, then routes added by the configuration are in error, as shown in Figure 6-7. If you click a route, you see an error message about the corresponding service's missing details.

Service Details

Traefik would need the server details for each service. In a microservice architecture, service registration is the process of adding all details to the registry. In our opinion, self-registration is the simplest possible mechanism that supports every possible scenario. We extend the self-registration to add Traefik specific details for the required Consul keys. The ServiceRegistry class accomplishes this responsibility.

```
@Configuration
public class ServiceRegistry implements ApplicationListener<Ser
vletWebServerInitializedEvent> {

    final String serviceKey = "/traefik/http/services/{0}/
    loadBalancer/servers/";
    final String serverKey = "/traefik/http/services/{0}/
    loadBalancer/servers/{1}/";
    final String urlKey = "/traefik/http/services/{0}/
    loadBalancer/servers/{1}/url";

    @PreDestroy
    void removerServerMapping() {
        if(index > -1) {
            consulClient.deleteKVValues(format(serverKey,
            applicationName, index));
        }
    }
}
```

177

```
void addServerMapping(int port)  {
    Response<List<String>> keys = consulClient.getKVKeysOnly
    (format(serviceKey, applicationName));
    index = keys.getValue()!=null ? keys.getValue().size() : 0;
    consulClient.setKVValue(format(urlKey, applicationName,
    index), format("http://{0}:{1,number,#}/","127.0.0.1",port));
}

// REMOVED for Brevity
}
```

The preceding code does the following.

- Determines the port on which the application is started

- Adds the host and port information to the Consul KV store by using ConsulClient

- Adds the values to the Traefik keys /traefik/http/ services/{0}/loadBalancer/servers/{1}/url

- Removes the keys at service shutdown

The ServiceRegistry class is part of every service. If you start all services and reload the dashboard, you see that all the errors are fixed. (see Figure 6-8)

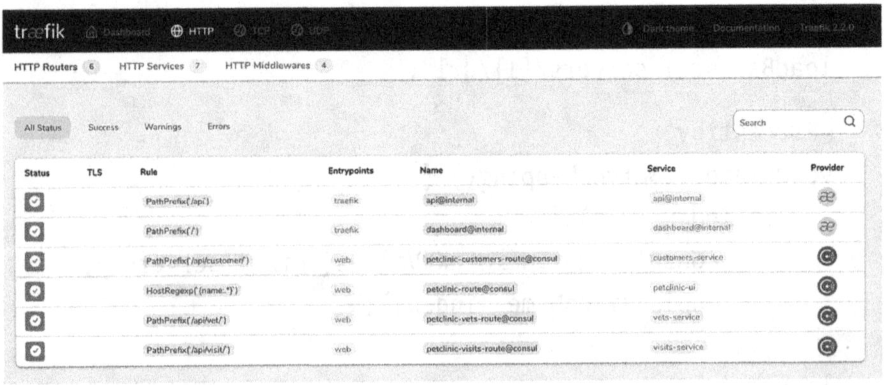

Figure 6-8. *PetClinic configuration*

> **Note**   Traefik continues to watch values in the KVS store. It
> automatically reloads the configuration as it is updated in Consul.

Now let's load the PetClinic application on http://localhost/. The
application performs as expected. We can load and save data across the
three different microservices. (see Figure 6-9)

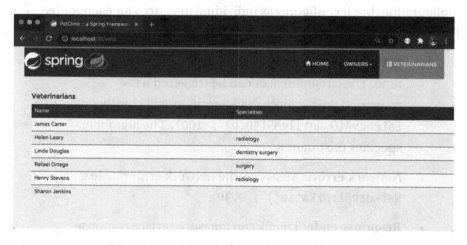

Figure 6-9. *PetClinic*

Circuit Breaker

We said that microservices often collaborate to deliver a complete user
function. A service invokes other services to get relevant data. But in a
distributed system like microservices, the remote service call can hang for a
while before failing. An unresponsive service call blocks the resources from
the calling service. If there are many of these calls, the system may run out of
critical resources leading to cascading failures across multiple systems.

A circuit breaker is often applied to address this problem with fail-fast behavior. The circuit breaker tracks remote calls. In an unhealthy response, the circuit breaker returns immediately without sending the call to the destination service. This book does not cover the pattern in detail.

Traefik provides middleware that can configure a circuit breaker. Since the circuit breaker is configured as part of the middleware chain, the circuit breaker only alters the behavior after its execution. It is important to note that even though the circuit breaker is declared once in the configuration, but it configures as individual instances for each route. Traefik can detect service error rates in the following metrics.

- **Latency**: Traefik can measure service quantile latency time. The circuit breaker can be triggered if the measured time is more than a configured value (e.g., `LatencyAtQuantileMS(50.0) > 100`). The argument specifies the quantile.

- **Network errors**: Measures the network error rate (e.g., `NetworkErrorRatio() > 0.30`).

- **Response code**: Traefik can measure service response status codes (e.g., `ResponseCodeRatio(500, 600, 0, 600) > 0.25`). The four arguments here are HTTP status codes.

  - Error status code From

  - Error status code To

  - Application Status code From

  - Application Status code To

Each of these metric values can be checked by using the following operators.

- Greater than (>)

- Greater or equal than (>=)

- Lesser than (<)

- Lesser or equal than (<=)

- Equal (==) and

- Not Equal (!=) operators

You can also combine two or more metrics using AND (&&) and OR (||) operators. When Traefik determines that a circuit breaker has been triggered, it does not forward the call to the destination service; instead, it returns a 503 response. (see Figure 6-10)

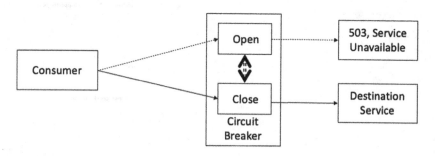

Figure 6-10. *Traefik circuit breaker*

Let's now add the following response status circuit breaker to over services.

```
$ consul kv import "$(cat circuitbreaker.json)"
Imported: traefik/http/middlewares/response-check/
          circuitbreaker/expression
Imported: traefik/http/routers/petclinic-customers-route/
          middlewares/1
```

We added circuit-breaker middleware for the customer-service route to the configuration. The circuit breaker is triggered when customer service returns 500 error code. Traefik also shows the circuit breaker middleware configuration on the dashboard. (see Figure 6-11)

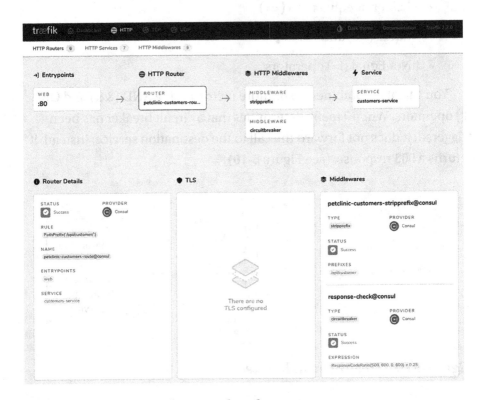

Figure 6-11. Route with circuit breaker

Retries

In a dynamic ecosystem, service instances can be in a starting state. There can be intermittent network connectivity errors. These transient errors are generally self-correcting. If you retry the service call, chances are it will succeed. Retry is another mechanism that makes an application fault tolerant.

The retry pattern states that you can retry a failed request. It is important to identify which failures may work with this approach. If the application reports an invalid data error, then the chances are high that it does not work on retry. Additionally, a failed request propagated throughout the system creates unnecessary bottlenecks. On the other hand, if a request has failed due to the connection or a response timeout, chances are high that it will succeed if retried.

Traefik supports the retry pattern by using retry middleware, which reissues request a specified number of times to a service if there are timeout errors. The middleware stops reissue as soon as there is a response from the service. The middleware done validates if the response received is erroneous. We can add retry middleware configuration and enable it for routes in the following manner.

```
$ consul kv import "$(cat retry.json)"
Imported: traefik/http/middlewares/retry-check/retry/attempts
Imported: traefik/http/routers/petclinic-vets-route/middlewares/1
```

We configured the retry middleware for four retries. The middleware is applied to the vets-service route in the configuration. It is difficult to test such a configuration. The configuration is applicable when the service is slow to respond. The error is only replicated in-case of connection timeouts. These are actual network errors. The retry mechanism does not kick in for request timeouts. In these cases, the request is processing by the service, but the processing can be very slow. Such requests, if retried, can cause unintended issues, like dual debit in account debit requests.

Retries can only work properly if there are configured timeouts in Traefik. This is a global level configuration. Traefik provides serversTransport.forwardingTimeouts static configuration attributes that can control the timeouts to the servers.

- idleConnTimeout: Specifies the maximum amount of time an idle connection remain idle before closing

- responseHeaderTimeout: Specifies the amount of time to wait for a server's response headers

- dialTimeout: Specifies the time spent establishing a connection

```
serversTransport:
  forwardingTimeouts:
    responseHeaderTimeout: 1s
    dialTimeout: 1s
    idleConnTimeout: 1s
```

We configured one-second timeouts for service response and idle connection in the configuration. Let's restart Traefik and validate the retry middleware configuration on the dashboard.

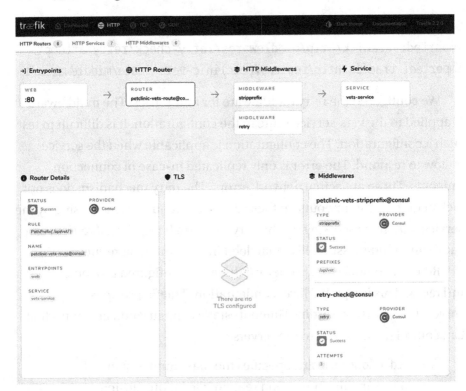

Figure 6-12. *Route with retry*

The configuration shows that three retries are performed for a failed request.

Throttling

In a microservice architecture, different services collaborate to deliver user value. This involves applying enterprise integration techniques to applications to address various issues. One of the common issues in application integration is about controlling the consumption of resources. Some of the resources are expensive to create, so their access must be moderated with service level agreements. Throttling is the method that controls misbehaving or rouge services by sending more requests than the service level agreement. It is essential to apply this to a critical-section service as the complete ecosystem stall if the critical-section service fails. This can help improve application capacity planning.

Throttling is often implemented by rejecting overflowing requests. Traefik supports throttling by using rate-limit middleware. It can measure average calls within a defined period from a particular source. The middleware sends HTTP status 429 (too many calls) to the source service if it invokes calls more than the configured limit. The middleware provides the following three attributes to configure the API rate.

- **Average**: Counts the number of requests in the configured period

- **Period**: Specifies the time (the rate is defined as the average calls/period)

- **Burst**: Specifies how to handle the maximum request within a short time

There are options to control the source identification. We can enable the rate-limit middleware for the vets service.

```
$ consul kv import "$(cat ratelimit.json)"
Imported: traefik/http/middlewares/ratelimit-check/ratelimit/
          average
Imported: traefik/http/middlewares/ratelimit-check/ratelimit/
          period
Imported: traefik/http/routers/petclinic-vets-route/
          middlewares/2
```

Traefik updates the configuration and shows it in the dashboard, as shown in Figure 6-13.

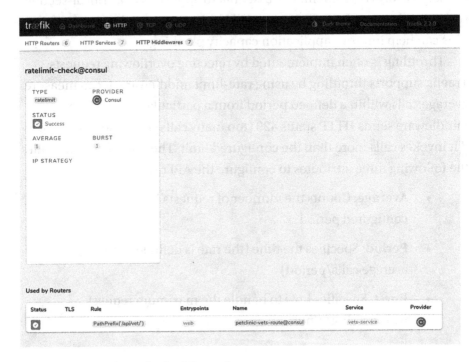

Figure 6-13. *Throttle dashboard*

We defined the rate as 1 request/30 seconds. If we try to make a couple of requests for /api/vets/vets, you see the following response.

```
Request URL: http://localhost/api/vet/vets
Request Method: GET
Status Code: 429 Too Many Requests
Remote Address: [::1]:80
Referrer Policy: no-referrer-when-downgrade
```

Middleware Chain

Traefik provides a chain middleware that can be used to simplify configurations applied across different services. The chain middleware can be used to group middleware in order. The complete group can be applied to a route, removing the need to apply each middleware separately. The complete chain is specified by providing a comma-separated list to the chain middleware attribute. In this scenario, we can configure the chain to consist of the circuit breaker and rate limit middleware.

```
$ consul kv import "$(cat chain-list.json)"
Imported: traefik/http/middlewares/chain-list/chain/middlewares
Imported: traefik/http/routers/petclinic-customers-route/
          middlewares/0
```

Traefik updates the configuration and shows it in the dashboard, as shown in Figure 6-14.

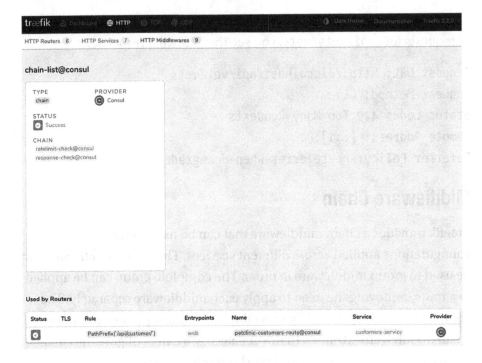

Figure 6-14. *Chained middleware*

Canary Deployments

Traefik supports Canary deployments using weighted round-robin.
In the previous section, we added the ServiceRegistry class to add
instance details. These instances are used in a round-robin manner. In
Chapter 3, we discussed the weighted round-robin, where weights were
added to server instances. Traefik divides received requests in the ratio
of the provide weights. As we start new instances, you see new services in
the Consul service registry (see Figure 6-15). Weight can be added from
the UI for each instance.

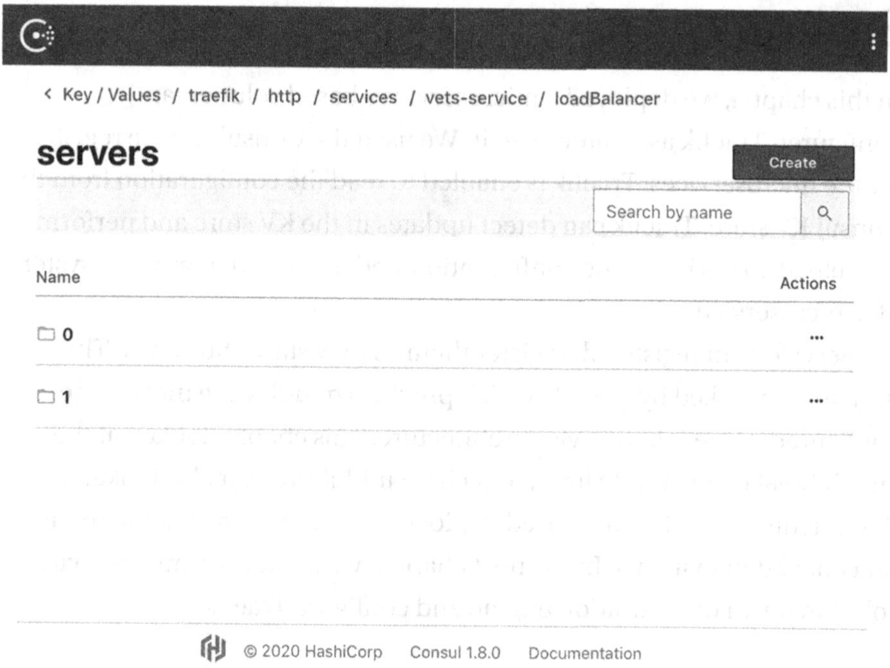

Figure 6-15. *Multiple instances*

Redirecting a subset of requests to a new service is one of the fundamental foundations for canary deployments. The mechanism can be automated by using a Consul client. But the complete end-to-end flow needs additional components which can provision and deploy the newly released version.

Note   This chapter integrated Traefik with the Consul KV store. Traefik also provides integration with Zookeeper and etcd. Configuration with others is similar to Consul-based integration, but some features do not work as expected.

Summary

In this chapter, we deployed a microservices-based solution and configured Traefik as a gateway to it. We used the Consul service registry for the microservices. Traefik is enabled to read the configuration from the Consul KV store. Traefik can detect updates in the KV store and perform hot reloads. This keeps the configuration updated in a dynamic ecosystem like microservices.

Services can register/deregister them as they start/shutdown. These updates are picked by Traefik, which provides middleware that can be configured in the microservice architecture. This chapter looked at the circuit breaker, retry, rate limit, and chain middleware. It also looked at the weighted round-robin-based deployment, which can split the requests for canary deployments. In the next chapter, we deploy the microservices solution on an orchestration engine and configure Traefik.

CHAPTER 7

Traefik as Kubernetes Ingress

In this final chapter, you try out Traefik's native integration with the Kubernetes container orchestration platform. Kubernetes is undoubtedly the most popular container microservices platform. Traefik integrates tightly with Kubernetes and can act as a first-class citizen in the Kubernetes ecosystem. You already tried out Traefik's many gateway capabilities. This chapter explores how easily these capabilities map to Kubernetes ingress concepts. You also see Traefik's simple integration with Jaeger, a Kubernetes-specific distributed tracing solution.

Note As in previous chapters, the focus remains on how Traefik integrates with the Kubernetes ecosystem, rather than its advanced features. We assume that you have a basic familiarity with Kubernetes primitives, and so we restrict our explanations on how Traefik maps to them.

Traefik as Kubernetes Ingress Controller

Kubernetes is primarily an orchestrator/scheduler and an API server that supports the desired state configuration. Typically, clients submit declarative YAML resource requests to the Kubernetes API server, and

Kubernetes accordingly provisions the requested resources. For each such resource type supported by the Kubernetes API server, such as deployment or service, a default Kubernetes controller acts on and provisions the submitted resource request. The one exception is the *ingress* resource type.

The Ingress object defines the traffic routing rules (e.g., load balancing, SSL termination, path-based routing) in a single resource to expose multiple services outside the cluster. According to the official Kubernetes documentation:

> *Ingress is a collection of rules that allow inbound connections to reach the endpoints defined by a backend. An Ingress can be configured to give services externally-reachable URLs, load balance traffic, terminate SSL, offer name-based virtual hosting, etc.*

This is not very different from how Traefik acts as an API gateway. An *ingress controller* is a component responsible for provisioning the submitted ingress requests. Kubernetes does not ship with a default ingress controller. Third-party vendors provide implementations. There is a reference (and widely used) nginx-ingress-controller based on Nginx (there are three different versions of it), but end users are free to deploy any other ingress controller they like. In this chapter, we make a case for Traefik as an ingress controller of choice.

Traefik has supported the Ingress API in earlier versions. But in Traefik v2 they have made some changes to the method of configuration. This is due to limitations in the Ingress API, which have plagued the specifications.

Ingress API specification spent a long time in beta. It has been in v1beta1 status since Kubernetes version 1.2. The specification was officially finalized only in 2019 and attained GA status in Kubernetes version 1.19. The basic specification is fairly simple, but there were challenges in making a consistent standard across a wide variety of implementations. There is no good way to pass in vendor-specific configurations to fine-tune for specific implementations. Implementors started to define vendor-specific configuration in lots of custom annotations in the YAML definitions, leading to fragmentation in the space. Older versions of Traefik followed the same approach. There have also been ambiguities such as a trailing '/' handled inconsistently (and problematically). Ultimately, the specification is imprecise and neither portable nor feature-rich, so the original intent of having a standard API was never achieved. Many third-party vendors didn't adopt the ingress specification and used LoadBalancer service type with their own custom configuration—again through annotations. Ambassador API Gateway built ingress support in 2019, once the specification was finalized.

Most of the Kubernetes community has now moved away from custom annotations (for other use cases as well), and the ingress specification, and toward *custom resource definitions* (CRDs). A CRD defines a new object Kind in the cluster and lets the Kubernetes API server handle its lifecycle. Kubernetes is a system open for an extension, allowing external implementors to define their custom resource API definitions and run custom controllers to act on those custom API resources.

The third-party ingress implementations retooled to act as Kubernetes controllers for the CRDs they defined. Contour was one of the first ingress API gateways to introduce its CRD for configuration. Even Ambassador Gateway now recommends using its own CRDs rather than the new ingress support. Traefik followed suit, and Traefik v2 introduced the IngressRoute (and other) CRDs to provide a nicer way to configure Traefik routes in Kubernetes.

Traefik has two separate providers for Kubernetes now. One is the traditional Kubernetes ingress provider, where Traefik acts exactly like any other Kubernetes ingress controller and uses many custom annotations. The other is the Kubernetes CRD provider, which is our focus for this chapter. All the ingress configuration for Traefik is submitted to Kubernetes using Traefik's IngressRoute and other CRDs. This provides a much nicer experience in configuring Traefik on Kubernetes and is the recommended approach at present.

Note   Throughout this chapter, the word service is overloaded. The common meaning of service is an application that exposes an API, which is how we used the term in general. There is also service in the context of the Traefik configuration, which points to an actual backend service. In this chapter, there is also a Kubernetes Service, which is how Kubernetes routes traffic to pods. To avoid confusion, we explicitly spell out the meaning of all occurrences.

Installation of Traefik on Kubernetes

For this chapter, we are running a local Kubernetes cluster on a laptop for Traefik installation and configuration. The installation of local Kubernetes is beyond the scope of this book, but it should not be too complicated to set up from official websites. We variously use microk8s (`https://microk8s.io/`) (running over multipass on macOS) or minikube (`https://minikube.sigs.k8s.io/docs/`) for different scenarios.

Microk8s makes the setup of some advanced Kubernetes applications very trivial, while minikube is the de-facto standard for running a local version of Kubernetes. You may prefer to use any other Kubernetes flavor you like, such as Docker Desktop with Kubernetes enabled. You can use a cloud-based managed offering as well. And, we shift to a managed cloud offering for a couple of the later scenarios.

We expect no changes needed in Traefik configuration and installation between local and cloud Kubernetes. The reason for using a cloud offering is for working with public TLS certificates again (similar to Chapter 4). For TLS termination using Let's Encrypt, we provision a cloud Kubernetes cluster on DigitalOcean (DOKS). You may prefer to use others such as GKE, AKS, or EKS if you desire. Most of the steps we outline should just work as-is on any Kubernetes distribution.

We already have our local Kubernetes cluster running. All requests to the Kubernetes API server happen through the kubectl CLI, which is typically installed along with local Kubernetes distros. Kubectl needs a kube context configuration to point to our target Kubernetes cluster. We first install Traefik manually on our cluster. Then we explore an easier installation mechanism in later sections. In order to get Traefik up and running on Kubernetes, we need three pieces of configuration.

- Kubernetes RBAC configuration to give Traefik sufficient permissions to talk to the API server.

- Traefik CRDs

- The actual Traefik deployment

Note   These are standard Traefik deployment files. We encourage you to get the updated versions of all of these from the Traefik documentation at `https://docs.traefik.io/providers/kubernetes-crd` and `https://docs.traefik.io/routing/providers/kubernetes-crd`.

Listing 7-1. Installing Traefik RBAC via kubectl

```
# First install the RBAC security configuration
% kubectl apply -f traefik-rbac.yml
clusterrole.rbac.authorization.k8s.io/traefik-ingress-
controller created
clusterrolebinding.rbac.authorization.k8s.io/traefik-ingress-
controller created

# RBAC configuration details, full configuration omitted for brevity
rules:
  - apiGroups:
```

```
      - ""
    resources:
      - services
      - endpoints
      - secrets
    verbs:
      - get
      - list
      - watch
  - apiGroups:
      - extensions
    resources:
      - ingresses
    verbs:
      - get
      - list
      - watch
  - apiGroups:
      - extensions
    resources:
      - ingresses/status
    verbs:
      - update
  - apiGroups:
      - traefik.containo.us
    resources:
      - middlewares
      - ingressroutes
      - traefikservices
      - ingressroutetcps
      - ingressrouteudps
```

```
      - tlsoptions
      - tlsstores
   verbs:
      - get
      - list
      - watch
```

Again, Kubernetes provides a declarative API server, so the RBAC configuration in Listing 7-1 grants Traefik read permissions to Kubernetes Services and on its custom resources under the `traefik.containo.us` API group (even though we did not install the CRDs yet). Traefik can watch objects of these types for changes and reconfigure itself accordingly. Next, we install the Traefik CRDs in Listing 7-2.

Listing 7-2. Installing Traefik CRDs via kubectl

```
% kubectl apply -f traefik-crd.yml
customresourcedefinition.apiextensions.k8s.io/ingressroutes.
traefik.containo.us created
customresourcedefinition.apiextensions.k8s.io/middlewares.
traefik.containo.us created
customresourcedefinition.apiextensions.k8s.io/ingressroutetcps.
traefik.containo.us created
customresourcedefinition.apiextensions.k8s.io/ingressrouteudps.
traefik.containo.us created
customresourcedefinition.apiextensions.k8s.io/tlsoptions.
traefik.containo.us created
customresourcedefinition.apiextensions.k8s.io/tlsstores.
traefik.containo.us created
customresourcedefinition.apiextensions.k8s.io/traefikservices.
traefik.containo.us created
```

```
# IngressRoute CRD
apiVersion: apiextensions.k8s.io/v1beta1
kind: CustomResourceDefinition
metadata:
  name: ingressroutes.traefik.containo.us

spec:
  group: traefik.containo.us
  version: v1alpha1
  names:
    kind: IngressRoute
    plural: ingressroutes
    singular: ingressroute
  scope: Namespaced

# Rest omitted for brevity
```

We install 7 CRDs as listed in Listing 7-2. These are all the CRDs Traefik ships with for different types of custom configuration. This number may increase in the future. Instead of picking and choosing, we just installed all of them. We listed the IngressRoute CRD, which is used heavily in upcoming sections. The specific details are not very interesting. The CRDs need to be installed so Traefik can keep a watch for any Custom Resource requests of these types to the API server and act on it. Traefik is acting as the Kubernetes controller, which operates on these custom resource types. As per the listing, there is a different CRD for each different type of Traefik specific configuration. This is a big advantage that the new CRD approach gives us. Earlier, a lot of this would have been defined as custom annotations on standard ingress resources.

Next, we install Traefik (see Listing 7-3). We are installing Traefik as a Kubernetes deployment with one pod. Kubernetes keeps at least one instance of Traefik running at all times. Since Traefik is a stateless service and all configuration is coming from Kubernetes, even if the pod is restarted, Traefik retains the configuration.

Listing 7-3. Traefik Installation via kubectl

```
% kubectl apply -f traefik.yml
serviceaccount/traefik-ingress-controller created
deployment.apps/traefik created
service/traefik created
```

Just with that, Traefik is now installed and running on our cluster. In the context of Kubernetes, there is no difference between installing an application and running it. It automatically starts up within a container. Let's take a look at some of the deployment configuration in Listing 7-4.

Listing 7-4. Traefik Deployment Configuration

```
# Many fields omitted for brevity
kind: Deployment
metadata:
  name: traefik
spec:
  replicas: 1
  template:
    spec:
      containers:
        - name: traefik
          image: traefik:v2.2 #the Traefik Docker image used
          args:
            - --log.level=DEBUG
            - --api.insecure
            - --api.dashboard
            - --entrypoints.web.address=:80
            - --entrypoints.traefik.address=:8080
            - --providers.kubernetescrd
          ports:
```

```
      - name: web
        containerPort: 80
      - name: traefik
        containerPort: 8080
kind: Service
metadata:
  name: traefik
spec:
  type: NodePort
  ports:
    - protocol: TCP
      port: 80
      name: web
      targetPort: 80
    - protocol: TCP
      port: 8080
      name: traefik
      targetPort: 8080
```

We listed some partial configuration in Listing 7-4 for the Traefik deployment and service. You can see the image version to be deployed and the number of replicas. Traefik runs as a stateless service with state managed by Kubernetes, so there is no problem running multiple replicas as desired for scale-out (since it does not have to form a stateful cluster).

The interesting part is the static configuration. The dynamic Traefik configuration is all provided at runtime by the Kubernetes provider, including Traefik routes and Traefik services. However, the static configuration—such as entrypoints and providers—still has to be provided at startup time. Traefik leverages the usual CLI parameters approach for this. This is the usual way to pass Traefik static configuration for Docker and Kubernetes. We start with two entrypoints here: one for HTTP traffic and the other for the dashboard. We also expose the dashboard in insecure mode since we are running locally and set the log to the desired level. This is all typical stuff.

The new flag is the `--providers.kubernetescrd` value. This ensures that Traefik can configure itself based on the Kubernetes CRDs. The subtle catch is that it only picks up the new Traefik-based CRDs. If you also want Traefik to act as the standard Kubernetes ingress controller, you must pass the `--providers.kubernetesingress` flag. You can enable either one or both providers. You also expose the Traefik ports themselves, so Kubernetes can register them. Don't forget Traefik is exposed outside the cluster as a Kubernetes Service of type NodePort. The service is shown in Listing 7-5.

Listing 7-5. Traefik Kubernetes Service

```
% kubectl get svc traefik
NAME      TYPE        CLUSTER-IP      PORT(S)
traefik   NodePort    10.110.30.69    80:31624/TCP,8080:32529/TCP
```

Irrespective of which Kubernetes worker node(s) Traefik is running on (locally, we just have one), Kubernetes forwards any incoming traffic on the exposed NodePorts on any of the worker nodes to the running Traefik instance(s). If there are multiple Traefik pods, Kubernetes automatically load balance requests among them. This is the usual Kubernetes behavior for the NodePort service type. In the cloud scenario, we would instead have used the LoadBalancer type for the Traefik service, which spins up a cloud load balancer to expose the Traefik service, and all requests to Traefik go through the load balancer IP. The cloud platform operates the load balancer. Locally, we usually use NodePort though some local Kubernetes distributions also support LoadBalancer now through special mechanisms.

Let's now look at the default Traefik backend on the port 31624 exposed by Kubernetes (see Figure 7-1). This port is randomly allocated by Kubernetes and may be different. This forwards the request to Traefik's web entrypoint on HTTP port 80. Since there is no default route configured for this entrypoint, we get a 404 as usual. Please note the IP address is the local IP of the minikube VM, which can be accessed using the minikube ip command.

Figure 7-1. *Default backend on NodePort entrypoint*

We also exposed the Traefik dashboard on the other port to check out the configuration (see Figure 7-2). There are two entrypoints configured: traefik and web. The traefik entrypoint serves the dashboard route, while web is meant for all other HTTP traffic. Please note Traefik documentation recommends not to expose the dashboard in insecure mode in actual production use. Chapter 4 covered how to expose the dashboard securely over TLS. For local use, it is fine for now to access it this way.

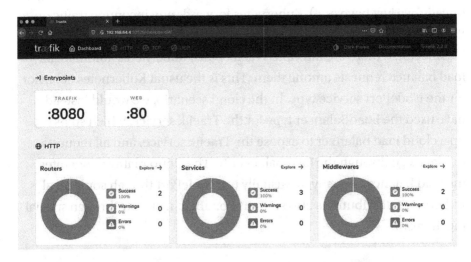

Figure 7-2. *Traefik deployment with dashboard entrypoint*

If you scroll down to the Providers section, you see that the Kubernetes CRD provider is enabled (see Figure 7-3). In earlier chapters, we used the FileProvider and the Consul provider. The old Kubernetes ingress provider is not enabled, so Traefik does not act on standard ingress resources.

Figure 7-3. *Traefik deployment with Kubernetes CRD provider*

Next, we deploy a Kubernetes service on our cluster and try accessing it through the `traefik` entrypoint.

Installing the bookinfo Application

Now that Traefik is up and running, let's deploy a microservices style application to our cluster, which can be exposed over Traefik. For this, we use the BookInfo sample application from the Istio documentation (`https://istio.io/latest/docs/examples/bookinfo/`). This application is composed of a few different containerized microservices, and while it is primarily a showcase for the Istio service mesh, we can use it for Traefik.

Please note we could have also used the Spring PetClinic application from the previous chapter. However, at the time of writing, that application is not fully Kubernetes native yet. We have to make adjustments to run it on top of Kubernetes. BookInfo is built to run on top of Kubernetes so we can focus directly on the post-deployment parts. We are not interested in its actual code. After deployment, the only service to be exposed over Traefik is the main web app, called `productpage`.

The web app calls the rest of the services internally. There are many different deployment configurations for BookInfo. We are only interested in basic deployment. This file is at `https://github.com/istio/istio/blob/master/samples/bookinfo/platform/kube/bookinfo.yaml`. You can download it or apply it directly with the raw URL (see Listing 7-6).

Listing 7-6. Install bookinfo Services

```
% kubectl apply -f bookinfo.yml
service/details created
serviceaccount/bookinfo-details created
deployment.apps/details-v1 created
service/ratings created
serviceaccount/bookinfo-ratings created
deployment.apps/ratings-v1 created
service/reviews created
serviceaccount/bookinfo-reviews created
```

```
deployment.apps/reviews-v1 created
deployment.apps/reviews-v2 created
deployment.apps/reviews-v3 created
service/productpage created
serviceaccount/bookinfo-productpage created
deployment.apps/productpage-v1 created
```

Once the deployments and services are up, we can proceed to apply the IngressRoute. This is pretty standard. It just exposes all the paths which the web app needs to call from the browser. We must create our own to work with Traefik. We can then access the BookInfo application on the HTTP web NodePort. First, let's look at which of BookInfo's Kubernetes services are available (see Listing 7-7).

Listing 7-7. BookInfo Services

```
% kubectl get svc
NAME            TYPE        CLUSTER-IP        PORT(S)
details         ClusterIP   10.111.105.145    9080/TCP
productpage     ClusterIP   10.101.6.99       9080/TCP
ratings         ClusterIP   10.102.103.167    9080/TCP
reviews         ClusterIP   10.103.10.20      9080/TCP

% kubectl get deploy
NAME              READY   UP-TO-DATE    AVAILABLE
# 3 separate reviews deployments, rest omitted for brevity
reviews-v1        1/1     1             1
reviews-v2        1/1     1             1
reviews-v3        1/1     1             1
```

Listing 7-7 is a bunch of services created of type ClusterIP. This means they can talk to each other but are not reachable outside of the cluster. The only one we must expose using IngressRoute is the productpage service. This is the main web app of BookInfo and serves requests on port 9080.

We can apply an IngressRoute custom resource for this service to expose it over Traefik. Let's first take a look at some of the configuration of this resource in Listing 7-8. You can see that it broadly matches our usual dynamic configuration defined via FileProvider. There is an entrypoint defined and route with the usual match rules. The interesting part is the section where the backend service configuration typically goes. Here you see that we refer directly to a Kubernetes service and Traefik route to it. So, the IngressRoute more or less defines a Traefik route from an entrypoint to a backend Kubernetes service. If needed, we can also reference Traefik middleware here.

Listing 7-8. BookInfo IngressRoute

```
spec:
  entryPoints:
    - web
  routes:
  - match: PathPrefix(`/productpage`) || PathPrefix(`/static`)
|| Path(`/login`) || Path(`/logout`) || PathPrefix(`/api/v1/
products`)
    kind: Rule
    services:
    - name: productpage
      port: 9080

% kubectl apply -f bookinfo-product-ingress.yml
ingressroute.traefik.containo.us/bookinfo-productpage-ingress
created

% kubectl get IngressRoute
NAME                              AGE
bookinfo-productpage-ingress      29s
```

Once the service is exposed on the Ingress, we can easily view the webpage (see Figure 7-4). This internally calls the other BookInfo services to populate data on each part of the page. This webpage may look slightly different on each request as the reviews service is backed by three different reviews deployments (as shown in Listing 7-7).

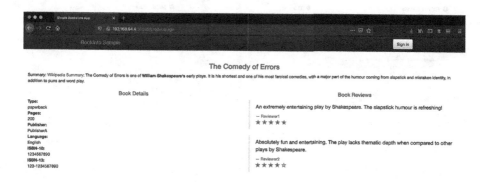

Figure 7-4. *BookInfo product page UI*

We can now check the configuration in the Traefik dashboard. You see the routers and services configuration showing up. The IngressRoute has automatically created a router and a service (the Traefik abstraction, not the Kubernetes one, though they are the same in this case). The Kubernetes service is automatically discovered by Traefik and treated as service abstraction in Traefik. You can see the router and service information in the dashboard shown in Figures 7-5 and 7-6.

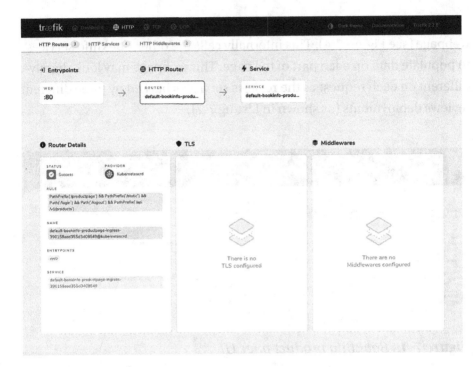

Figure 7-5. *Product page router*

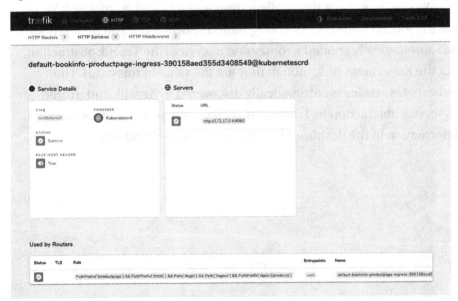

Figure 7-6. *Product page ingress service*

If you explore the servers in the service configuration (where we typically define the load balancer IPs of the backend service), you see the pod IPs of the corresponding Kubernetes service (see Figure 7-6). Traefik can automatically introspect those details from Kubernetes and deal with the internal Kubernetes network (it would need to). When there is any change in the pods (e.g., scale up or down, pod restarts, etc.) that the Kubernetes service is pointing to, Traefik automatically picks it up. This raises an interesting point of contrast with the last chapter. There, we had to integrate Traefik with the Consul service registry using the Consul provider to keep track of the services. However, Kubernetes provides service discovery out of the box, and Traefik can directly talk to Kubernetes to fetch the service details.

Note   LoadBalancer in this context refers to the Traefik configuration for specifying multiple backend service IPs and not the Kubernetes LoadBalancer.

In case it has not been made clear yet, this example illustrates how IngressRoute is the CRD style implementation of a Traefik HTTP router. This is the advantage of using the CRD approach over the plain Ingress, it allows you to stick more closely to Traefik-style configuration.

Installing Traefik with Helm

In the previous section we successfully deployed Traefik on Kubernetes and used it to expose a service. There were a few different manual steps involved with just basic configuration. With more advanced Traefik configuration, the manual steps required can quickly become unwieldy, especially if we want to adjust the static configuration over time or do regular upgrades of Traefik. For production installation, we instead use a package and release manager called Helm (`https://helm.sh/`) to install Traefik on Kubernetes. In Helm, a deployable artifact is bundled up into a chart that encapsulates all the resources necessary to install and upgrade that software over time, including configuration and dependencies. There is a Traefik Helm chart that we use from now to install/upgrade Traefik. Helm reuses the current kubeconfig set by kubectl. We already have the latest version of Helm v3 installed and our kubeconfig setup to point to our local Kubernetes cluster.

The version of Traefik available in the central Helm repositories (similar to Maven central, PyPi, or the Debian apt repositories) is the older Traefik v1.7 version. Accordingly, we need to run a couple of advance steps before installing Traefik v2 via Helm (see Listing 7-9). These register the Traefik v2 Helm repository so we can install Traefik v2 using Helm. Make sure that you do not accidentally install the older version; it does not support the IngressRoute CRDs and works somewhat differently.

Listing 7-9. Adding Traefik's Helm repository

```
% helm repo add traefik https://containous.github.io/traefik-
helm-chart
"traefik" has been added to your repositories

% helm repo update
Hang tight while we grab the latest from your chart
repositories...
...Successfully got an update from the "traefik" chart
repository
Update Complete. ☼ Happy Helming!☼
```

Once this is done, we can go ahead and install Traefik v2 using its official Helm chart. Since we already installed Traefik manually, we need to either reset the entire cluster (easily done on minikube) or remove everything installed until now. Let's do a fresh install now.

Exploring Traefik Helm Chart

The Traefik Helm chart installs all the pre-requisites needed to run Traefik as an ingress controller, including the Kubernetes RBAC configuration and the CRDs to configure routing rules. The installation works the same way on either local or cloud Kubernetes with one exception. In a managed cloud service, Traefik ingress is exposed to the external world using a Kubernetes service of type LoadBalancer. This automatically spins up a managed cloud load balancer in front of all the Kubernetes nodes and routes all incoming traffic to the Traefik ingress controller. For the external world, the single point of entry is the IP or DNS name of the cloud load balancer.

A load balancer is not available on bare metal or on-premise VMs. Minikube and microk8s can handle this through a special mechanism, though it is usually simpler to use a NodePort. You need to ensure that your Kubernetes distribution of choice supports services of type LoadBalancer. If not, you must fall back to exposing the Traefik ingress as a Kubernetes service of type NodePort. This has to be taken care of during the Helm installation, by customizing the Helm chart values. This can be done by passing them on the command line to Helm, or a better way is to define a file for custom values which can override the default values during installation.

Let's look at some default values on the Helm chart (https://github.com/containous/traefik-helm-chart/blob/master/traefik/values.yaml) and then some that we want to customize (see Listing 7-10).

Listing 7-10. Some of the Default Values in Traefik Helm Chart values.yaml

```
# Configure the deployment with number of pods
deployment:
  replicas: 1
```

```yaml
# IngressRoute for the dashboard will be installed
ingressRoute:
  dashboard:
    enabled: true
# Configure both types of dynamic Traefik providers
providers:
  kubernetesCRD:
    enabled: true
  kubernetesIngress:
    enabled: true
# Configure ports
ports:
  traefik:
    port: 9000
            # As recommended, the dashboard is not exposed by
            default in production
    expose: false
# The HTTP and HTTPS ports are opened by default
  web:
    port: 8000
    expose: true
  websecure:
    port: 8443
    expose: true

service:
  enabled: true
  type: LoadBalancer
rbac:
  # False value indicates Traefik can be used cluster-wide
  across all namespaces.
  namespaced: false
```

This is not a standard Kubernetes manifest of any kind. These are just configuration values in YAML format applied to the Kubernetes YAMLs in the Helm chart. By default, it has the following configurations.

- One instance of Traefik runs in a Kubernetes pod

- Traefik service is exposed via a LoadBalancer. This may not work on a non-cloud cluster.

- Both the old and the new dynamic configuration Kubernetes providers are enabled. So Traefik keeps a watch for both standard ingress and Traefik's custom IngressRoute resource.

- Three entrypoints are opened: one named `traefik` on 9000, and two others for HTTP and HTTPS traffic. We explore the additional entrypoint a little bit more later.

- An IngressRoute custom resource for the dashboard is automatically created. However, the dashboard entrypoint is not exposed to the Traefik Kubernetes service. This is a little inconsistent and confusing because Traefik recommends creating your own secure ingress for the dashboard in production. However, we can leverage this IngressRoute locally in a little bit. This behavior is not documented anywhere we can find, so it may change in the future.

There are many such entries in the default values.yaml in the Helm chart. We encourage you to explore further configuration on their own. Most of it is related to running Traefik reliably on Kubernetes. For instance, autoscaling of Traefik pods under load is not enabled; it can be turned on if required. Please note these observations are for the current state of the Helm chart when writing this book. The chart continues to evolve.

Before we customize the values, we can use the `helm template` command to view the default generated deployment manifests. These are very similar to what we used to manually install Traefik in previous sections. Let's run the command to see what the final configuration looks like. Since there is a lot of output, we only focus on a few pieces. You are encouraged to run the command yourself to view the full output (see Listing 7-11).

Listing 7-11. Generated Helm Template with Default Values

```
% helm template traefik traefik/traefik

# Partial values in the output
# Deployment configuration
     #Kubernetes liveness probe
      readinessProbe:
        httpGet:
          path: /ping
          port: 9000

     #Kubernetes liveness probe
      livenessProbe:
        httpGet:
          path: /ping
          port: 9000

     # Traefik CLI arguments
      args:
        - "--entryPoints.traefik.address=:9000/tcp"
        - "--entryPoints.web.address=:8000/tcp"
        - "--entryPoints.websecure.address=:8443/tcp"
        - "--api.dashboard=true"
        - "--ping=true"
        - "--providers.kubernetescrd"
        - "--providers.kubernetesingress"
```

```
# Service configuration
  type: LoadBalancer
  ports:
  - port: 80
    name: web
    targetPort: "web"
    protocol: "TCP"
  - port: 443
    name: websecure
    targetPort: "websecure"
    protocol: "TCP"
# IngressRoute
kind: IngressRoute
metadata:
  name: traefik-dashboard
spec:
  entryPoints:
    - traefik
  routes:
  - match: PathPrefix(`/dashboard`) || PathPrefix(`/api`)
    kind: Rule
    services:
    - name: api@internal
      kind: TraefikService
```

Let's break down what we captured in Listing 7-11. The static configuration is provided via CLI arguments as usual. We already noted the three entrypoints and the two providers. You can also see the dashboard enabled flag. You also see that the ping Traefik service is enabled. We look at it in the dashboard later; it is exposed to the traefik port under the /ping path. It provides a standard way for Kubernetes to regularly check the health of the Traefik pods. If the health probes fail, Kubernetes automatically restarts the Traefik pods. This provides a resilient way to run Traefik on top of Kubernetes.

You see an IngressRoute `traefik-dashboard` created to expose the dashboard outside the cluster. This does not work in the default installation. The reason is the `traefik` entrypoint port 9000 is not included in Traefik's service configuration. While it is accessible inside the cluster for health checks, it is not available over the NodePort, and there is no way to reach that entrypoint to access the dashboard.

To customize some of the default values at install/upgrade time, we can override them in our file and provide that to the Helm CLI. Let's look at the values we want to customize in Listing 7-12. While the dashboard is not exposed publicly in production, here we override the configuration of the `traefik` entrypoint to make the dashboard available locally. We change the Traefik service to NodePort type, and we also set the log level to INFO. As you saw, the Traefik static configuration is still provided with CLI arguments. The Helm chart exposes a `additionalArguments` special key to pass in additional arguments.

Listing 7-12. custom-values.yml for Traefik Helm Chart

```
additionalArguments:
  - "--log.level=INFO"
ports:
  traefik:
    expose: true
service:
  type: NodePort
```

Let's run the Helm template command once again to view the generated deployment manifests with the custom values. We only list the new/modified values in Listing 7-13. This uses the same `custom-values.yml` file we detailed in Listing 7-12.

Listing 7-13. Generated Helm Template with Custom Values

```
% helm template --values=custom-values.yml traefik traefik/
traefik

# Partial changed values in the output
# Deployment configuration
        # Traefik CLI arguments
        args:
          - "--log.level=INFO"

# Service configuration
   type: NodePort
   ports:
   - port: 9000
     name: traefik
     targetPort: "traefik"
```

We are now able to access the Traefik dashboard outside the cluster with this configuration. Let's proceed to install Traefik.

Local Installation

Before installing Traefik, there is the additional question of which Kubernetes namespace we wish to install Traefik in. In production, the kube-system namespace is a good candidate if Traefik is responsible for cluster-wide ingress concerns. It resides along with the other cluster management/operational services. Another approach may be to restrict Traefik to only a particular namespace and use a different ingress controller (or a different Traefik deployment) for the rest of the cluster. The Helm chart supports it out of the box with the rbac.namespaced configuration. We stick with the default namespace for our examples.

Let's now install Traefik with the Helm command (see Listing 7-14). We reuse the same custom-values.yml file we detailed in Listing 7-12. We then run a few commands to observe it was properly deployed. Since the dashboard port 9000 is now exposed over NodePort, you can also open the dashboard (see Figure 7-7).

Listing 7-14. Install Traefik Using Helm

```
% helm install --values=custom-values.yml traefik traefik/
traefik
NAME: traefik
LAST DEPLOYED: Wed Apr 22 00:26:27 2020
NAMESPACE: default
STATUS: deployed
REVISION: 1
TEST SUITE: None

% helm ls
NAME       NAMESPACE   REVISION   STATUS     CHART           APP
VERSION
traefik    default        1       deployed   traefik-8.9.1   2.2.5

% kubectl get pods
NAME                          READY   STATUS     RESTARTS   AGE
traefik-5bcf58d556-vfhlv 1/1          Running       0        63s

% kubectl get svc traefik
NAME      TYPE       CLUSTER-IP     PORT(S)
traefik NodePort 10.99.103.150 9000:31342/TCP,80:30085/
TCP,443:30615/TCP

% kubectl get svc traefik -o yaml
spec:
  clusterIP: 10.99.103.150
```

```
    externalTrafficPolicy: Cluster
    ports:
    - name: traefik
      nodePort: 31342
      port: 9000
      protocol: TCP
      targetPort: traefik
    - name: web
      nodePort: 30085
      port: 80
      protocol: TCP
      targetPort: web
    - name: websecure
      nodePort: 30615
      port: 443
      protocol: TCP
      targetPort: websecure
    selector:
      app.kubernetes.io/instance: traefik
      app.kubernetes.io/name: traefik
    sessionAffinity: None
    type: NodePort

% kubectl get IngressRoute traefik-dashboard -o yaml
apiVersion: traefik.containo.us/v1alpha1
kind: IngressRoute

spec:
  entryPoints:
  - traefik
  routes:
  - kind: Rule
```

```
match: PathPrefix(`/dashboard`) || PathPrefix(`/api`)
services:
- kind: TraefikService
  name: api@internal
```

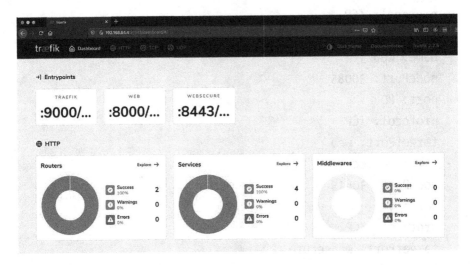

Figure 7-7. *Entrypoints with Helm install*

You can see our three entrypoints in the dashboard in Figure 7-7. You can also drill down to Routers and see the route mappings to Traefik's internal dashboard and ping services. The name of the routers may be of interest. For the `ping@internal` service, it is as usual. However, the dashboard IngressRoute pointing to `api@internal` has a generated name (see Figures 7-8 and 7-9). This is because there is a separately defined IngressRoute for it. A similar naming convention is used for all the IngressRoute objects defined.

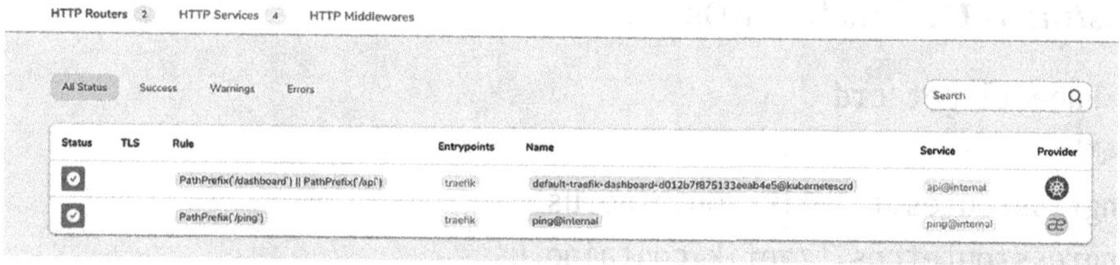

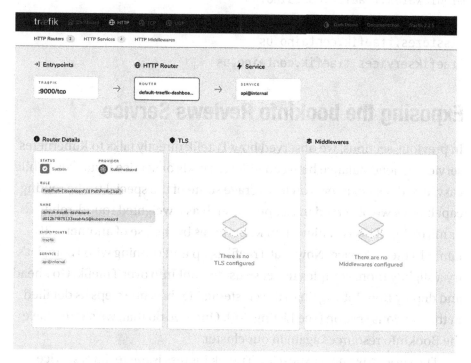

Figure 7-8. *Routes with Helm install*

Figure 7-9. *dashboard route*

The Helm chart also installs all the requisite Traefik CRDs. Traefik piggybacks on the standard Kubernetes declarative configuration mechanism to configure itself through these CRDs. There is a different CRD for each piece of dynamic router configuration. Let's look at what's installed in Listing 7-15.

Listing 7-15. Traefik CRDs

```
% kubectl get crd
NAME
ingressroutes.traefik.containo.us
ingressroutetcps.traefik.containo.us
ingressrouteudps.traefik.containo.us
middlewares.traefik.containo.us
tlsoptions.traefik.containo.us
tlsstores.traefik.containo.us
traefikservices.traefik.containo.us
```

Exposing the bookinfo Reviews Service

In previous sections, we observed how Traefik directly talks to Kubernetes services to load balance between different pods or service instances. While easy, this does not allow you to leverage some of the special traffic routing capabilities we observed in Chapter 3, such as a weighted round-robin or mirroring. This is achieved on Kubernetes by the use of another CRD named TraefikService. Now that Traefik is up and running with Helm, let's try a slightly more complex use case using BookInfo over Traefik. Go ahead and deploy BookInfo again to the cluster using the same steps as detailed in the previous section (see Listing 7-6). Once we do that, we should have the BookInfo resources again in our cluster.

The service we now expose on Traefik ingress is the reviews service. The productpage backend internally calls it. This is a single Kubernetes service that's backed by three separate deployments. The reviews service routes traffic to three pods, which all behave slightly differently.

- reviews-v1 returns a sample review.

- reviews-v2 calls the ratings service and returns a black color sample rating.

- `reviews-v3` calls the ratings service and returns a red color sample rating.

We expose this service using an IngressRoute while utilizing a Traefikservice. This allows you to try out the weighted round-robin strategy with the Kubernetes provider. Once the services are up, we can proceed to apply the IngressRoute. First, we create three additional Kubernetes service for the three separate deployments (see Listing 7-16). A Traefikservice has to point to existing Kubernetes services.

Listing 7-16. Three Separate Reviews Services

```
apiVersion: v1
kind: Service
metadata:
  name: reviews-noratings
  labels:
    app: reviews
    version: v1
    service: reviews
spec:
  ports:
  - port: 9080
    name: http
  selector:
    app: reviews
    version: v1
---
apiVersion: v1
kind: Service
metadata:
  name: reviews-black
  labels:
```

```
    app: reviews
    version: v2
    service: reviews
spec:
  ports:
  - port: 9080
    name: http
  selector:
    app: reviews
    version: v2
---
apiVersion: v1
kind: Service
metadata:
  name: reviews-red
  labels:
    app: reviews
    version: v3
    service: reviews
spec:
  ports:
  - port: 9080
    name: http
  selector:
    app: reviews
    version: v3

% kubectl apply -f bookinfo-reviews-extsvcs.yml
service/reviews-noratings created
service/reviews-black created
service/reviews-red created
```

```
# We now have 4 reviews services, one from the original deployment
% kubectl get svc
NAME                TYPE        CLUSTER-IP        PORT(S)
reviews             ClusterIP   10.110.252.89     9080/TCP
reviews-black       ClusterIP   10.97.126.88      9080/TCP
reviews-noratings   ClusterIP   10.111.136.174    9080/TCP
reviews-red         ClusterIP   10.105.94.3       9080/TCP
```

Once these services are in place, let's define a Traefikservice to apply a weighted round-robin strategy on two of them (see Listing 7-17). We club the reviews-black and reviews-noratings services together with 3:1 weightage.

Listing 7-17. 3 TraefikService Resources

```
apiVersion: traefik.containo.us/v1alpha1
kind: TraefikService
metadata:
  name: reviews-v1v2
spec:
  weighted:
    services:
      - name: reviews-black
        port: 9080
        weight: 3
      - name: reviews-noratings
        port: 9080
        weight: 1

% kubectl apply -f bookinfo-reviews-traefikservice.yml
traefikservice.traefik.containo.us/reviews-v1v2 created
```

We now apply an IngressRoute to expose these services externally (see Listing 7-18).

Listing 7-18. Reviews IngressRoute

```
apiVersion: traefik.containo.us/v1alpha1
kind: IngressRoute
metadata:
  name: bookinfo-reviews-ingress
spec:
  entryPoints:
    - web
  routes:
  - match: PathPrefix(`/reviews`)
    kind: Rule
    services:
# We can define multiple services here for simple Round robin
load balancing
    - name: reviews-v1v2
      kind: TraefikService
    - name: reviews-red
      port: 9080

% kubectl apply -f bookinfo-review-ingress.yml
ingressroute.traefik.containo.us/bookinfo-reviw-ingress created

% kubectl get IngressRoute
NAME                        AGE
bookinfo-review-ingress     29s

# Call reviews ingress on loop
% for ((i=1;i<=20;i++)); do curl http://192.168.64.5:30680/
reviews/1 | jq ; done
```

If you call the service ingress on a loop (see Listing 7-18), you see
the load is distributed among the three separate instances based on the
weightage provided. We get more review responses with red and black

ratings than ones with no ratings. You can view these services and routers in the dashboard in Figures 7-10, 7-11, 7-12, and 7-13.

Figure 7-10. *Generated ingress service*

Figure 7-11. *All reviews services in Traefik*

default-reviews-v1v2@kubernetescrd

ℹ️ Service Details		⊕ Services		
TYPE	PROVIDER	Name	Weight	Provider
weighted	🛞 Kubernetescrd	default-reviews-black-9080	3	🛞
STATUS		default-reviews-noratings-9080	1	🛞
✅ Success				

Figure 7-12. *Weighted Traefikservice*

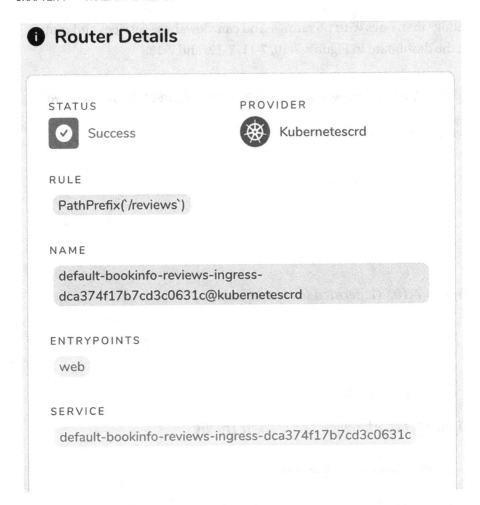

Figure 7-13. *Router for ingress service*

Configure Request Tracing with Jaeger

Chapter 5 showed how to integrate Traefik into a distributed tracing setup with Zipkin. While Zipkin has been the default choice for distributed tracing with the Spring Cloud ecosystem for several years, in the Kubernetes world, people prefer to use Jaeger (`www.jaegertracing.io`).

Jaeger is a CNCF distributed tracing system released by Uber that distributes tracing for your services running on Kubernetes. Jaeger is meant for large scale deployments and supports OpenTracing and other standards. The basic concept behind it is pretty much the same as Zipkin. It propagates trace headers to downstream services and aggregates spans based on all the data sent to a collector. Jaeger is the default tracing backend for Traefik. If we enable request tracing and don't specify anything else, Traefik automatically assumes Jaeger tracing.

Before proceeding with Jaeger configuration in Traefik, we need a running Jaeger instance. Jaeger's full setup is extensive and outside the book's scope. (A minimal setup on DigitalOcean cloud requires at least four Kubernetes worker nodes.) For demo purposes, Jaeger ships an AllInOne image, which packages all the components in a single executable and uses in-memory storage to be deployed in a single pod. The setup of this requires deploying a Jaeger operator and associated CRD. Similar to Traefik's CRD, when we submit a resource of type Jaeger to Kubernetes, it spins up the AllInOne Jaeger pod. You are encouraged to pursue this approach if you wish to dive deeper into Jaeger setup on minikube.

We are taking an even simpler approach to setup Jaeger for our example, which avoids all the complexities mentioned. We switch from minikube to microk8s, another local Kubernetes distribution. We install Traefik on it using our existing Helm chart and then enable Jaeger on microk8s (see Listing 7-19). This automatically deploys jaeger-operator and spin up a simple jaeger all-in-one deployment, without any manual effort on our end. We can then figure out which service endpoint to configure in the startup configuration. We are only interested in a couple of ports on a particular service: one TCP and one UDP (see Listing 7-19).

Listing 7-19. Enable Jaeger on microk8s

```
% microk8s enable jaeger

% microk8s kubectl get pod
NAME                                READY    STATUS
jaeger-operator-7b58b969cf-vh8pp    1/1      Running
simplest-658764ffff-xktbp           1/1      Running

% microk8s kubectl get svc simplest-agent
NAME             TYPE        PORT(S)
simplest-agent   ClusterIP   5775/UDP,5778/TCP,6831/UDP,6832/UDP
```

Jaeger specific configuration has to be specified along with request tracing configuration at startup time. Since we already have Traefik running on our cluster we can adjust the configuration and run a `helm` upgrade command. This spins up a new Traefik pod with tracing enabled and remove the existing one. We make following additions in our custom-values.yml file (see Listing 7-20).

Listing 7-20. Additions in custom-values.yml and Helm Upgrade

```
additionalArguments:
# New values in Helm configuration
  - "--tracing=true"
  - "--tracing.serviceName=traefik" # default value, can be omitted
  - "--tracing.jaeger=true" # default value, can be omitted
  - "--tracing.jaeger.samplingServerURL=http://simplest-
    agent:5778/sampling"
  - "--tracing.jaeger.localAgentHostPort=simplest-agent:6831"

% helm upgrade --values=custom-values.yml traefik traefik/traefik
```

You can check our dashboard and see that Jaeger tracing is enabled in Figure 7-14.

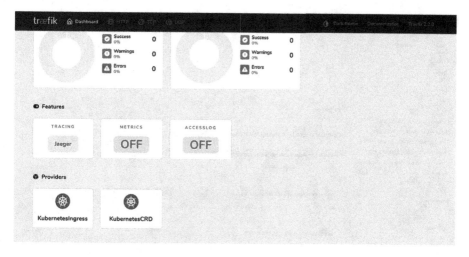

Figure 7-14. *Jaeger tracing enabled*

The following Jaeger configuration parameters are set by default.

- tracing.jaeger.samplingType=const

- tracing.jaeger.samplingParam=1.0

By default, this sends all traces to Jaeger. This can be tuned to control the volume of traces being sampled.

- tracing.jaeger.propagation=jaeger

This can be changed to send Zipkin-style traces, which Jaeger can interpret.

There are a few other configuration parameters in the documentation. The two required parameters that we need to set are already in the Helm configuration in Listing 7-20.

Since tracing is enabled globally, Traefik now starts sending traces for all incoming requests to the Jaeger collector. We can make a few requests and then check the Jaeger UI (see Figure 7-15).

Figure 7-15. *Jaeger traces on UI*

We can filter traces by the `serviceName` configuration we passed in to isolate the Traefik specific traces, and further by the Traefik entrypoints. We can drill down to a particular trace. The one in Figure 7-16 is for a request to the Traefik dashboard.

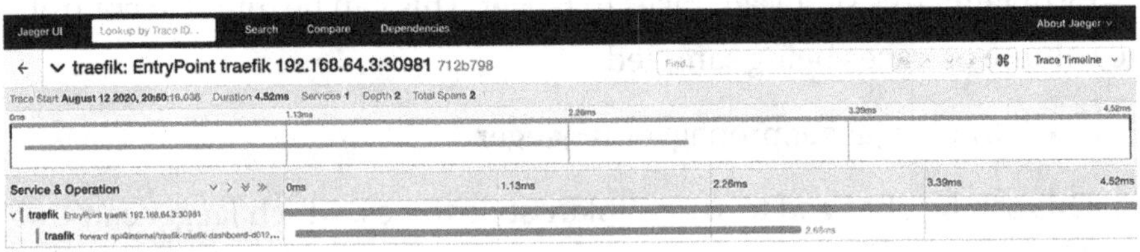

Figure 7-16. *Jaeger trace drill down*

There is one additional point of interest here. Since the Jaeger instance is running inside our cluster, how are we accessing the Jaeger UI? It needs to be exposed on a NodePort or via a Traefik ingress (or another ingress controller). Jaeger service setup by microk8s is exposing its UI as the default ingress rule in a cluster. One ingress (not IngressRoute) resource is present in the cluster, which was created automatically by the Jaeger operator (see Listing 7-21).

Listing 7-21. Jaeger UI Ingress on microk8s

```
% microk8s kubectl get ingress simplest-query -o yaml
kind: Ingress
spec:
  backend:
    serviceName: simplest-query
    servicePort: 16686
```

You have not encountered this format elsewhere in this chapter because you have not dealt with pure Kubernetes ingress resources. This defines a default backend for the default ingress controller, so if we hit the web/websecure entrypoints of our Traefik on root path (/), it opens up the Jaeger UI. You can view this in the Traefik dashboard, where it has configured a `default-router` for a `default-backend` (see Figure 7-17). There are two reasons for this behavior.

- The Traefik Helm chart sets up the Kubernetes CRD provider and the plain Kubernetes provider (as seen in Figure 7-14). If we disabled the old provider, this is not registered by Traefik.

- We do not have another ingress controller in this cluster. The default one is nginx-ingress-controller, but we have not enabled it. So Traefik is processing this ingress.

While this is not desirable behavior (it is just due to unforeseen variables and does not appear to be customizable or even documented), it is just for our example. It allows you to illustrate Traefik's support for Kubernetes ingress, which we skipped. This is not how it is set up in any real-world use case. The correct way is to expose the Jaeger UI via an IngressRoute object.

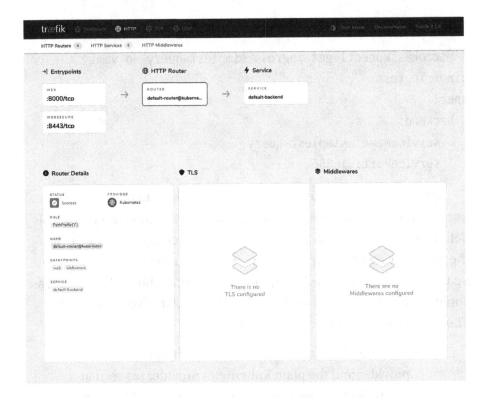

Figure 7-17. *Jaeger default ingress backend*

Setup Traefik on DigitalOcean Kubernetes Cloud

Let's now set up Traefik on DigitalOcean Kubernetes (DOKS). Anyone following along who wishes to use a different cloud provider can do so (AKS, EKA, GKE, etc). This is a cloud Kubernetes cluster managed by DigitalOcean. The actual provisioning of the cluster is beyond the scope of this book.

DigitalOcean makes it very easy via point-and-click actions. Once it is up, you get instructions on downloading the kubeconfig so that you can connect to your cluster using the local Kubernetes CLI (kubectl). For the cloud, exposing Traefik service as default type LoadBalancer on DOKS automatically provisions a cloud LoadBalancer for us. We only customize the log level for now during the Helm install in Listing 7-22.

From here on, kubeconfig has to be changed to point to our cloud cluster to execute all commands.

Listing 7-22. Install Traefik Using Helm on Cloud LB

```
# kubeconfig has to be changed to point to cloud cluster for
following commands
% helm install --set="additionalArguments={--log.level=INFO}"
traefik traefik/traefik

% kubectl get svc traefik
NAME      TYPE            EXTERNAL-IP     PORT(S)
traefik   LoadBalancer    139.59.53.243   80:30415/TCP,443:32494/TCP
```

DigitalOcean provisions a cloud load balancer. This process takes a little time, after which we get the public external IP to access our entrypoint (see Listing 7-22). Unlike NodePort, here we can route requests on the default ports. Recall that Traefik automatically generates a self-signed certificate for the HTTPS entrypoint, so you see what's shown in Figure 7-18 for port 443.

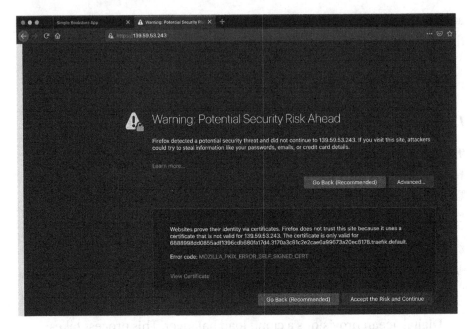

Figure 7-18. *HTTPS entrypoint with self-signed certificate on cloud load balancer*

When we proceed, we get the default backend for Traefik (see Figure 7-19).

```
404 page not found
```

Figure 7-19. *Default backend on cloud load balancer*

We do not expose the `traefik` endpoint for this deployment, so we cannot access the dashboard publicly. This is recommended in Traefik documentation. There are now two ways of viewing the dashboard. You can do either.

- Execute a `kubectl port-forward` command directly to the dashboard port. This restricts the dashboard access to only those having the kubeconfig (and perhaps services inside the cluster if they connect directly to the pod).

- Expose the dashboard with a secure IngressRoute as recommended by Traefik (similar to how we did it in Chapter 4).

TLS Termination on Kubernetes via Let's Encrypt Certificates

You've now seen the pieces needed to run Traefik on Kubernetes. The only thing not discussed yet is TLS support, which is necessary for any serious production use. Chapter 4 looked at how a publicly exposed Traefik instance can easily serve TLS traffic in conjunction with Let's Encrypt automated certificate distribution.

In Chapter 4, we exposed a secure route on Traefik running on a single cloud VM (or droplet) with basic auth enabled over a TLS connection (i.e., the `websecure` entrypoint. In this chapter, we try doing the same with Traefik on cloud Kubernetes. We deploy the BookInfo service and define an IngressRoute for it on the `websecure` entrypoint and request a valid TLS certificate from Let's Encrypt for that domain. Do recall that Let's Encrypt only issues a valid certificate for a publicly reachable domain. The domains of the issued certificate have to match the URL of the domain you are accessing for a valid TLS connection. To reconfigure Traefik with Let's Encrypt support, we provide a new values configuration file and upgrade our Helm release. We also change the log level to DEBUG (see Listing 7-23).

Listing 7-23. New cloud-values.yml file

```
additionalArguments:
  - "--certificatesresolvers.letsencrypt.acme.email=<valid email>"
  - "--certificatesresolvers.letsencrypt.acme.httpchallenge.
      entrypoint=web"
  - "--certificatesresolvers.letsencrypt.acme.storage=/data/
      acme.json"
  - "--certificatesresolvers.letsencrypt.acme.caserver=https://
      acme-staging-v02.api.letsencrypt.org/directory"
  - "--log.level=DEBUG"

persistence:
  enabled: true
  size: 1Gi    #min. volume size allowed on DigitalOcean
  storageClass: "do-block-storage"
```

We are using similar Let's Encrypt configuration here (see Listing 7-23) that we last used in Chapter 4, except now we are using CLI arguments instead of static YAML configuration. To mix it up, we use the HTTP-01 challenge instead of the TLS-ALPN-01 challenge. This is a more standard and widely used challenge type. It requires web entrypoint (port 80) to be publicly reachable (by Let's Encrypt).

We are using the Let's Encrypt staging URL as we don't care to get a valid production certificate. There is some extra configuration required for the storage location of the acquired certificate. Traefik's Helm chart provides this. Pods are generally transient and can't persist data to the pod filesystem without being backed by Kubernetes persistent volume.

A detailed discussion of Kubernetes storage abstraction is beyond our scope. The Traefik Helm chart provisions a storage location for writing data to the filesystem, which persist across pod restarts. The storage is mounted in the running Traefik pod at the /data location, and our acquired certificate is persisted in that folder. Without this, the certificate is lost on pod restart.

For reference, the storage configuration generated by the Helm chart looks like in Listing 7-24. This can be generated as usual by the Helm template command. It can be customized further in the Helm chart. The storage class `do-block-storage` attribute is vendor-specific. It is needed to provision storage in DigitalOcean, and it is not useful anywhere else.

Listing 7-24. Generated Storage Value Snippets

```
kind: PersistentVolumeClaim
metadata:
  name: traefik
spec:
  accessModes:
    - "ReadWriteOnce"
  resources:
    requests:
      storage: "1Gi"
  storageClassName: "do-block-storage"
# Additional Deployment configuration
spec:
  template:
    spec:
        volumeMounts:
          - name: data
            mountPath: /data
      volumes:
        - name: data
          persistentVolumeClaim:
            claimName: traefik
```

We can now do a helm upgrade to apply this configuration using the file from Listing 7-25.

Listing 7-25. Helm Upgrade with certresolver

```
% helm upgrade --values=cloud-values.yml  traefik traefik/traefik
Release "traefik" has been upgraded. Happy Helming!
NAME: traefik
LAST DEPLOYED: Sun Aug 16 20:34:16 2020
NAMESPACE: default
STATUS: deployed
REVISION: 2
TEST SUITE: None
```

At this point, we can deploy the BookInfo service using the exact same configuration as in Listing 7-6. We then define a new IngressRoute to reach this service. First, we open another terminal and tail the Traefik pod logs in Listing 7-26. Recall that we changed the Traefik log level to DEBUG. We can check the certificate acquisition process.

Listing 7-26. Secure Dashboard IngressRoute

```
# In a separate terminal
% kubectl get pod
NAME                       READY  STATUS
traefik-6cb8d56bf8-sghpj   1/1    Running

% kubectl logs -f traefik-6cb8d56bf8-sghpj
time="2020-08-16T15:07:37Z" level=info msg="Configuration
loaded from flags."
time="2020-08-16T15:07:37Z" level=info msg="Traefik version
2.2.8 built on 2020-07-28T15:46:03Z"
time="2020-08-16T15:07:37Z" level=debug msg="Static
configuration loaded...
...
```

Let's leave this running and move back to our main terminal to apply the IngressRoute (see Listing 7-27).

Listing 7-27. TLS IngressRoute for bookinfo productpage

```
# whoami-doks-ingress.yml
apiVersion: traefik.containo.us/v1alpha1
kind: IngressRoute
metadata:
  name: productpage-ingresstls
spec:
  entryPoints:
  - websecure
  routes:
  - match: Host(`k8straefik.rahulsharma.page`) && (PathPrefix
    (`/productpage`) || PathPrefix(`/static`) || Path(`/login`)
    || Path(`/logout`) || PathPrefix(`/api/v1/products`))
    kind: Rule
    services:
    - name: productpage
      port: 9080
  tls:
    certResolver: letsencrypt
```

```
#Apply the IngressRoute
% kubectl apply -f bookinfo-doks-ingress.yml
```

In the log tail terminal in Listing 7-16, you see messages in the log on applying the YAML and opening up the browser (see Listing 7-28). We are omitting a lot of information for brevity. We already added a subdomain entry in our public domain provider to point to our load balancer's IP address. You see that Traefik tries to first use the TLS-ALPN-01 challenge type and then falls back to the HTTP-01 challenge. The challenge is a multistep process that provides an automated response to Let's Encrypt on default HTTP port on our publicly reachable domain, which is why port 80 needs to be open for this challenge.

241

Listing 7-28. Lets Encrypt HTTP-01 Certificate Negotiation Log Snippets

```
level=debug msg="Try to challenge certificate for domain
[k8straefik.rahulsharma.page] found in HostSNI rule"
level=debug msg="Domains [\"k8straefik.rahulsharma.page\"]
need ACME certificates generation for domains \"k8straefik.
rahulsharma.page\"." providerName=letsencrypt.acme
level=debug msg="legolog: [INFO] [k8straefik.rahulsharma.page]
acme: Could not find solver for: tls-alpn-01"
level=debug msg="legolog: [INFO] [k8straefik.rahulsharma.page]
acme: use http-01 solver"
level=debug msg="legolog: [INFO] [k8straefik.rahulsharma.page]
The server validated our request"
level=debug msg="legolog: [INFO] [k8straefik.rahulsharma.page]
acme: Validations succeeded; requesting certificates"
level=debug msg="Certificates obtained for domains [k8straefik.
rahulsharma.page]"
```

When you access the BookInfo productpage URL in the browser you get the usual response and can inspect the staging certificate (see Figure 7-20).

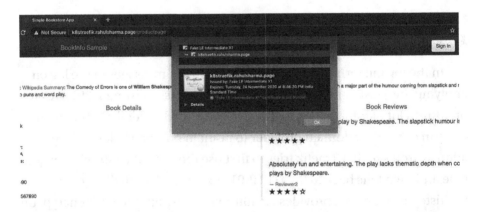

Figure 7-20. *BookInfo product page UI on cloud load balancer with LE certificate*

TLS Certificate Limitations with Multiple Traefik Instances

You may feel we are now ready to roll out Traefik to run on Kubernetes in production; however, there is one hitch. The point we didn't cover yet was high availability (HA). One of the good things about Kubernetes is that it provides HA support automatically by load balancing traffic between multiple pods of the same service. If autoscaling is enabled, Kubernetes horizontally scales-out further pods to handle an increase in requests.

This can apply to Traefik as well since it runs as a Kubernetes service backed by a deployment. This HA creates a problem for Traefik ACME protocol integration with Let's Encrypt. As you saw earlier, the automated Let's Encrypt TLS challenges require a multistep interaction. There is no way to guarantee that the same instance of Traefik receives all the challenge requests. Also recall that Traefik stores the dynamically acquired certificates in an acme.json file in a shared persistent volume.

The Traefik documentation warns you that this file should not be used for concurrent access by multiple instances. So, the Let's Encrypt integration breaks down when you scale Traefik horizontally. Traefik does not allow such a deployment configuration to proceed; it throws an error during Helm installation.

The commercial version of Traefik, TraefikEE, supports this distributed Let's Encrypt configuration. However, if we want to stick with the free community edition, this approach does not work. We can fall back to configuring manually acquired certificates as Kubernetes Secrets, then referencing it in our IngressRoute configuration, as shown in Listing 7-29.

Listing 7-29. TLS IngressRoute for Whoami

```
# whoami-doks-ingress.yml
apiVersion: traefik.containo.us/v1alpha1
kind: IngressRoute
metadata:
  name: productpage-ingresstls
spec:
  entryPoints:
    - websecure
  routes:
  - match: Host(`k8straefik.rahulsharma.page`) && PathPrefix
    (`/productpage`) || #etc..
    kind: Rule
    services:
    - name: productpage
      port: 9080
  tls:
    secretName: k8straefik-tls # TLS certificate already added
                                      as Kubernetes Secret
```

If we still want to use Let's Encrypt to automatically acquire and renew certificates, Traefik recommends using Jetstack cert-manager (https:// cert-manager.io). Cert-manager is the de-facto solution for managing certificates on Kubernetes. It uses ACME protocol the same as Traefik to provision certificates for different use cases, though it doesn't support the TLS-ALPN-01 challenge like Traefik. Cert-manager boasts native integration with Kubernetes Ingress. If we create a plain Kubernetes ingress resource and add the right custom annotation, cert-manager automatically provision a TLS certificate for the domain.

The catch is that at the time of writing, it doesn't work yet with Traefik's IngressRoute CRD. The Traefik team is working on this integration. As a workaround, for now, we can create a certificate custom resource for cert-manager, which acquire and save a certificate as a Kubernetes secret, and then manage the certificate thereon. This can be used in a IngressRoute resource exactly as in Listing 7-29. Since this is a workaround for a limitation that likely be resolved soon, we do not elaborate on it.

Summary

This chapter deployed and configured Traefik on top of Kubernetes using its Helm chart. Traefik has tight integration with Kubernetes, and its API gateway capabilities map easily to the Kubernetes Ingress. This makes it a very attractive proposition for use as an Ingress controller.

You tried out Traefik's native integration with Kubernetes in the form of CRDs. You saw how Traefik can detect dynamic updates in the Kubernetes API server and keep its configuration updated without any manual intervention. Services are registered and deregistered in Traefik as they are updated in the Kubernetes cluster.

While this chapter covered a lot of complex ground in a compressed time, this complexity is inherent to the Kubernetes ecosystem. In our view, Traefik simplifies the job of deploying and managing an API gateway on Kubernetes.

With that, we come to the end of this chapter and also this book. Traefik is rapidly evolving day by day, and we encourage you to head on over to the Traefik official documentation to continue your exploratory journey of Traefik.

Index

A

B

C

U, V

W, X, Y

Printed in the United States
By Bookmasters